"It is not so much what happens to you, but how you view the situation which, in turn, determines the consequences."

"The good news concerning the problem is that you are doing these things to yourself. That also means that you can stop doing them."

❖ ❖ ❖ ❖

"My own coping mechanisms had never been particularly appropriate to my needs. What sense had there been in recording every bite of food that went into my mouth? The food was not the problem, not anymore than my mouth was."

❖ ❖ ❖ ❖

"For all the years that I had felt badly about myself, I had managed to reinforce these feelings through a great many negative actions. But now that I felt good about myself, my actions had had to adjust themselves accordingly."

❖ ❖ ❖ ❖

Published by: Golden One Publishing
P.O. Box 44542
Phoenix, Arizona 85064-4542

© 1990 Dorie F. Pass R.D.
ISBN: 09625992-3-9

Cover Design: Skolos Wedell, Boston, Massachusetts
Cover Photo: Foto Foto, Phoenix, Arizona
Hair & Make-up: Mario Cobos, Salon Coupe, Scottsdale, Arizona

Everybody's Doing It...And Here's How to Quit

By Dorie F. Pass R.D.

Dedication

To KAREN—for teaching me what I needed to know, without which I would not be here today.

In Summary

For a period of sixteen years, I suffered from a severe eating disorder and chronic depression.

Throughout this time, I constantly berated myself for my inability to control either my weight or my moods. It did not occur to me that my binge-eating might be caused by anything more than an uncontrollable love for food. But then I learned that my overeating was merely a symptom of a much greater disorder—a *thinking* disorder that not only nurtured my compulsive eating habits, but also my low self-esteem, my self-hatred, and finally, my self-destructive behavior.

Although it is possible to alleviate all of the foregoing symptoms for short periods of time, non-functional thought patterns make it impossible to address the underlying problems.

Everybody's Doing It and Here's How to Quit was written both to reassure and also to assist those whose maladjustive thought patterns have caused them to believe that their problems are rooted in weakness or simply in a lack of will.

The moral of my own particular story is that diets may, in fact, NOT be the answer for an overweight person. At least not a permanent one.

Whatever the addiction, it nonetheless comes back to how we perceive ourselves and the world, and how successfully we are able to relate to the world in which we live.

It is my sincere hope that this book will prove helpful to those who are currently suffering under the misbegotten notion that nothing can be done because they are not strong enough or determined enough to do it. At the lowest point in my life, this faulty assumption was enough to put me in a mental institution. But correcting my maladjusted thought processes has provided the assurance that no such drastic "lows" will ever again occur.

Has my weight problem been cured? Yes.

Have I found it necessary to restrict myself to a diet in order to maintain my present weight? No.

There is no longer a desire to overeat, which enables me to eat whatever I wish.

In retrospect, it is easy to see that no diet could ever have provided the best means of approaching life and its constant challenges. My inability to approach them wisely and well resulted in a severe eating disorder. A diet was not the answer and would never have been.

Dorie F. Pass

Prologue

Even though most people experience occasional low moods, it would be inaccurate to say that they are severely depressed. This term has been bandied about with such carelessness that its real meaning is frequently misconstrued.

Depression is not simply a matter of "getting up on the wrong side of the bed." Nor can it be cured by getting up on the RIGHT side.

Severe depression, for those who may be wondering if they are actually afflicted with it, will cause one to feel out of control of their moods and thoughts. It makes a person unable to perceive anything other than the dark side of life.

Depressed people feel acute sensations of guilt and remorse. They frequently feel helpless in the face of relatively simple tasks, believing themselves incapable of actually performing such tasks. The most ordinary things—getting out of bed, brushing one's teeth, taking out the trash, etc., will be thought about and thought about by the depressed individual who finds it impossible to amass enough interest or energy to accomplish such chores.

Persistent symptoms of depression may include: unusual fatigue, anxiety, insomnia (or excessive sleep), changes in eating patterns, loss of sexual desire, withdrawal, phobias, feelings of hopelessness and guilt, and in the more advanced stages, a constant preoccupation with suicide.

It is wrong to believe that if you are able to somehow work AROUND these symptoms, or if you are able to disguise them in the company of others, that you are still "all right."

I can assure you from first-hand experience with all of these symptoms that *absolutely nothing* is all right. On the contrary, something—or possibly *everything*—is very definitely wrong. In my own case, over a period of sixteen years, I suffered with a severe eating disorder, and also, with such immobilizing periods of depression, that I found myself totally unable to function. It became impossible to get out of bed, to contemplate another day, to feign any interest in anyone or anything. There were frequent thoughts of suicide—and even with the aid of psychiatric counseling, and anti-depressant drugs, I could not seem to stabilize my moods, my behavior, or my life. Like so many others, I finally came to believe that my particular case was one—perhaps the ONLY one in the entire world—that was totally incurable.

It was at this lowest point that I finally found the answer to my problems. Incredibly, I found it inside myself, the one place where I had not thought to look.

Only eight months later, I would once again be happy and healthy—liberated and healed of all my earlier afflictions.

This, then, is my story. In presenting both the worst and the best of it, I would hope that others might be encouraged to seek the help that is needed, to persevere, and to always believe that an answer can be found.

1

October 1986

I will try to resolve to be better.
Only I can't.
I know I won't be.
I never am.

That morning in October, I decided to face up to things. For a very long time I had been fooling myself about getting better. About being a worthwhile person. About having a reason to go on with my life.

In the medicine cabinet were twenty-one librium tablets. Earlier, I had counted them and wondered if that would be enough. There was no one I could ask without arousing suspicion. Then I thought about the library.

"Yes ma'am, I'm writing this book—and well, there's a scene where this woman decides to kill herself. I thought she might do it with librium tablets. The thing is, I'm not sure about the dosage—how many it would take. I don't suppose a dozen would be enough—but maybe twenty would do it. Do you have any means of checking that out for me?"

I lay in bed and rehearsed my little speech, trying to sound casual—and non-suicidal. I found this

1

extremely difficult since suicidal was something I had been for a very long time. Suicidal, and bulimic, and given to prolonged and overwhelming fits of depression. For a period of sixteen years, I had struggled with these afflictions and tried to call it a life. But now I knew that it *wasn't* a life. What it had been was a form of imprisonment, to the extent that a person can become imprisoned within their own mind and body.

I hated my body because of the way it looked. I hated my mind because of the way it worked. Regardless of what I tried to do in an effort to improve my diet and appearance, my thoughts and feelings would always undermine me. Through the years, I had developed as many "inner controls" and "coping mechanisms" as it was possible to devise.

I had monitored my eating habits, every bite of food that went into my mouth. I had monitored my regimen for exercise, my fluctuations in weight, everything that could possibly have any affect upon my outward appearance. I had policed myself, chastised myself, punished myself, only to find myself binging again. Binging and sinking into yet deeper pits of depression.

I had never understood my pattern of behavior, nor had anyone ever been able to explain it to me. My childhood had been pleasant and carefree, my school years not unusually stressful. I was happily married, gainfully employed, and had every reason to feel good about myself. The irony was that so many people believed that I *did*. They did not realize that they were only seeing me on days when I could manage to drag myself out of bed, when I could somehow fashion a mood that was optimistic, even "bubbly". It took a gargantuan amount of effort to play the roles I felt others would find acceptable. Aware of their individual perceptions of me, I felt obliged to live up to them. Until the task became too great. Until the black shroud of melancholy enveloped me so totally that I could no longer shake it off.

That was the situation on October 17, 1986. It was my sister's anniversary. Although I knew she was expecting me to call, I could not bring myself to do it. Everything I thought about doing went no farther than my thoughts. It was the blackest mood I had ever experienced—but no, there had been another. On that particular day, I had attempted suicide.

Suddenly recognizing my symptoms for what they were, I managed to phone my doctor. He was not immediately available, and so I left a message asking him to call. I did not say it was an emergency. Whether or not I believed that it was, I did not feel comfortable with the idea of demanding anyone's attention. That had never been my style. I was much more comfortable with the role of trying to convince others that I had no problems at all. And throughout the month of September, I had been very convincing indeed.

It had been a month of such manic behavior that I hardly recognized myself. Rather suddenly, I wanted to accomplish everything at once.

There were many chores around the house that had been neglected. The most predominant one concerned itself with some painting that needed to be done.

A year earlier, some water pipes in the house had burst. After these pipes were replaced, the walls had been replastered. But the replastered walls had never been repainted. Although I had already lived with this situation for a year, I suddenly found that I could not tolerate it another instant. A painting contractor was immediately hired, and so, a major renovation project began.

For a period of several days I scrubbed and cleaned and rearranged furniture. I drove myself from daylight to dusk becoming increasingly meticulous as time went on, I even cleaned the corners of my windowsills with Q-tips. No small matter was ignored or overlooked.

Once the housework was done, I looked for other things to do. I learned that a movie was being filmed at a local health club. As one of its members, I had no trouble acquiring a small role in this film. I found it to be an exciting if somewhat physically exhausting experience.

On the heels of all this, I decided to go back to college. Although I had been thinking about it for some time, I had never been able to work up enough energy or desire to put this plan into action.

I contacted the enrollment office at Arizona State University and talked to them about a course in psychobiology. This study of the mental processes and their interrelationship with human anatomy and physiology had long interested me. I knew that chemical imbalances in the body could create problems such as I had experienced. In retrospect, I would have to say that I not only believed but secretly *hoped* that my problems were of a chemical nature. Perhaps vitamin supplements or a simple change in diet would be enough to lift that huge black cloud of despondency. The thought of acquiring a greater understanding of my chemically-based problems and possibly finding a solution for them was one that truly excited me.

As my high momentum in September gradually began to abate, a desperate attempt was made to alleviate the onset of yet another state of deep depression and the corresponding desire to binge. As my visits to the doctor became more frequent, additional thyroid medication was prescribed, together with another antidepressant and an anorexic drug to counter my tendency to binge. Although it was hoped that this new combination of pills would successfully ease my depression, by October 17, it hadn't happened. Instead, I was once again contemplating suicide.

One of the more curious aspects of this particular state of depression was the way in which I managed to battle through it with sudden bursts of energy. Although I had no intention of living out the day, I nonetheless felt compelled to keep an appointment I had made to have my hair cut. Once this was done, I returned home and crawled back into bed.

As the day advanced, my mood grew bleaker and more morose. The fact that the doctor had not called could only mean one thing. I was no longer a person worth calling. Perhaps I had never been.

As I wallowed in these and other dysfunctional thoughts, I made out a grocery list and subsequently went shopping. Quite aside from my own sinister plans, I still felt concern for my husband, Larry, who would be upset if he came home and found there was nothing to eat. It did not occur to me that he might be even more upset to find that his wife had taken her life.

By then, my logic was so twisted, so far removed from reality that it was difficult, if not impossible, to follow. I made no attempt to follow it. I simply acted on whatever whim was momentarily strong enough to motivate me. And so, my erratic behavior continued, gradually building to a crisis point. Then suddenly—the phone rang. Upon answering, I recognized the voice of my doctor.

All at once, I was engulfed in a panic attack of terrifying proportions.

"Oh God, Doctor, I don't know what to do!" I blurted out. "I've tried everything and I just can't come out of it."

"Out of what?" he asked, trying to make some sense out of my words and my mood.

"I don't know! Whatever this is. Whatever makes me the way I am. I hate myself and I try to change, but everything I do makes it worse."

"Now wait—let me see if I understand you here. Are you sick? Are you in pain?"

"I'm sick. I'm in pain. The pain is everywhere. It's all around me. It IS me. It's the only thing I feel. I just can't stand it anymore!"

"Are you alone?"

"Yes! Yes. I'm alone!" I cried, answering the question as I'd actually heard it. I sobbed hysterically at the thought of just how alone I really was.

In a way it would have been difficult to explain, I no longer felt connected to anyone. I was no one's wife, no one's child, no one's friend—certainly not my own. Somehow I had become separated from everyone and had drifted away into a kind of nameless void. While it had alarmed me at first, I had soon grown accustomed to it. And there had even been times

6

when I welcomed the opportunity to be free of having to relate to anyone. There was a burdensome responsibility connected with that.

By then, the dialogue within my marriage had deteriorated to a point where a minimum amount of words were being exchanged.

"How was your day?"

"Fine. Yours?"

"Fine."

"Good."

That was often all our dinner conversation consisted of, and because of the state I was in, I was actually glad!

What I suddenly found myself babbling out to the doctor was the most I had said in weeks. Coming all in a rush, it undoubtedly startled, even alarmed him. He was highly aware, as I was not, of the more common suicidal signs. The apathy I expressed, the desire to crawl into bed and hide, was one. Cutting one's hair was another. Giving away one's possessions was a third. During one of my regular visits, I had mentioned that it was only the menial errands and chores I felt obliged to do that somehow kept me functioning.

"What must you do today?" he had asked.

"Return a department store purchase. I've decided I don't want it."

"Maybe you should keep it," he had immediately suggested. "Later on, you might change your mind."

Despite my doctor's advice, I had returned the item, never once suspecting the true nature of his concern. But now I could clearly hear it in his voice.

"I think you should be hospitalized," he said.

7

While I was inclined to agree, I no longer believed that any local facility could provide the help I needed.

My doctor and I discussed the possibility of my being admitted to either the psychiatric medical facility at UCLA, or to the McLean Psychiatric Hospital in Boston. In view of the fact that my family was living in the Boston area, I felt that McLean's might not be the best choice.

"On the contrary, it would be a good choice," my doctor insisted. "You can't do this alone, Dorie. You're going to need a support system."

After we had talked a while, I understood and agreed. Even in the midst of my emotional trauma, I felt good about having made this decision. Finally, I was doing something I truly wanted and needed to do.

After calling my parents and tearfully advising them of the news, I angrily confronted my husband, who was late in coming home. I recounted the events of that day as if I were talking to someone who was totally indifferent to my problems, although I knew he was burdened with a difficult and challenging schedule. Larry's professional expertise lay in the field of gastroenterology, and at that time he was working hard to build a successful practice.

I told him how sad and unhappy I was, and that I was leaving for Boston. I told him about some new tests that could analyze my brain waves and determine if anything was wrong.

"My psychiatrist and I agreed upon McLean's," I said, "so that's where I'm going. I've already called my parents. The arrangements have all been made."

Larry listened to all I had to say, secretly relieved that I had chosen to take this step. Later, he would confide in my brother, Ken, that his growing concern for me had begun to affect his work.

"Each day when I come home, I find myself wondering how she'll be—even *who* she'll be," he said. "During the past two weeks, while she was spiraling down, I've been afraid of what it might lead to. I've had all kinds of crazy thoughts. I'm so glad she's finally agreed to get help. I know it will make a difference."

Throughout our marriage, Larry had frequently suspected that things were not entirely right with me. He had seen my weight fluctuate wildly, had known I was capable of being highly exhilarated, but also, deeply depressed. At times, he had even joked about my "manic depressive" ways, but the constant demands upon his time had not permitted him to dwell upon the things that might be wrong with me. Even so, he wondered about them, and through the years, had grown increasingly concerned.

The wonder of it is that we managed a fairly normal relationship, perhaps because I was able to conceal so much for so long. When Larry was not home he had no way of knowing how much I ate, or how often I slept the entire day away. He was not subjected to many of my moods, and I could generally 'contrive to be happy' for the few hours we were actually together. Since we did not communicate often or well, a few quick words would see me through the evening. Larry inevitably had other things to do or think about—and, of course, so did I. We co-existed in a climate of mutual acceptance. He was there. I was there. And that was all there was.

9

On the morning Larry took me to the airport, I made him promise not to tell anyone where I was going or why.

"I won't," he said, "but it's nothing to be ashamed of."

While I had fully expected him to say this, I was nonetheless embarrassed. But there was also something else. To tell others was to *involve* others, if only through their sympathy and support. I was determined to do this alone.

I boarded the plane with a certain degree of optimism, convinced that this was a major turning point in my life. This was to be the end of my emotional peaks and valleys, the end of all temporary solutions to my problems. With the knowledge that I had reached the very depths of suicidal despair came the encouraging realization that there was no way to go but up.

Upon take-off, I actually felt as if the plane and I were one—both soaring up, up and beyond the restricting bonds of earth.

The passenger seated next to me was an Italian woman traveling to Boston to visit with her sister. She spoke with great affection for the past, reminiscing about earlier childhood days. I found myself wondering how this friendly, outgoing woman would feel if she knew she were seated next to someone who was about to be admitted to a mental institution. Had she asked, how could I possibly have described the nature of that tiny invisible quirk that separated me from her and everyone else on board? It hardly seemed possible that any of this could be happening.

Only sixteen years earlier, as a student at Cambridge Junior College, I had been an entirely different person. I had been happy, carefree, and hopelessly optimistic. That was the way I had seen myself, that was the image I projected. But now I began to wonder about it.

In September of 1971, as a naive eighteen-year-old, I gave little thought to why I was going to college, or what I hoped to accomplish there. It seemed to me that life had a certain unalterable pattern. A person went to school, they graduated, pursued some professional endeavor, got married, had children, and eventually died.

For reasons I could not possibly have explained, it never occurred to me to question this pattern, or to deviate from it.

I adjusted well to college life. I made friends easily, got along with my roommate, and did well in all of my classes. Life was an easy, uncomplicated succession of days that were fun-filled and challenging.

But there was also a problem. I had begun to gain weight. By Thanksgiving of my freshman year, I had outgrown most of my clothes. Those I could still struggle into were extremely tight and unflattering.

I returned home during the holiday break, feeling awkward, sluggish and extremely unattractive.

"Never mind. It happens sometimes," my mother insisted, once the family had taken note of my altered appearance. "It's a different routine. A different lifestyle. That can lead to a different sort of diet."

It was felt that better eating habits and increased exercise to offset so many sedentary hours of

11

study was all that was needed to make me slim and trim again. No consideration was given to the actual source of the problem since we all believed that this had already been established. The problem was too many calories. The solution was to eat a bit less.

With all best intentions, I quickly found I was unable to control my periodic binging. It came as something of a shock. Each time I failed, I grew depressed at my failure, and my depression would cause me to binge.

Believing it was only determination that I lacked, I began to police my own activities. I purchased a calorie counter with the thought that I must evaluate every bite of food that went into my mouth. I subsequently read somewhere that the consumption of a single teaspoon of sugar (in any form) was enough to set back a weight reduction plan by three days.

Actually, it was a relief to learn that sugar was the enemy. I concluded that if I avoided sugar and ate very little, the problem would soon be overcome.

Returning to school, I found myself immersed in a number of coping mechanisms, which included avoiding food as much as I possibly could. I kept very little of it around, and frequently skipped breakfast and lunch, thereby enabling myself to feel more entitled to dinner. Dinner was generally a sparse and colorless meal, deliberately concocted to engender very little enjoyment or appeal. Determined to break what I believed to be my great "love affair" with food, I felt it would be best to eat things that didn't look or taste particularly appetizing.

As all self-denial systems go, it worked for a while. I managed to lose some weight and felt more in control of things. But then suddenly, everything came undone. Without any reason or warning, I found myself binging again. Over a period of time, it became quite common for me to drop ten or fifteen pounds in a matter or weeks, and then quickly gain back twenty.

Each time this happened, I grew more frustrated and angry. I constantly berated myself for my weak and undisciplined character. I would find myself binging to get over the depression that came with the binging that came with being depressed.

Whatever this was—this treacherous and never-ending cycle—it continued to ensnare me. No longer able to explain my compulsive behavior, I sought valiantly to conceal it. And so began a pattern of lies deliberately contrived to mislead almost everyone I knew.

After telling my roommate that I had started on a diet, I would sometimes find myself secretly devouring an entire box of cookies.

"Why are you eating that ice cream cone?" she asked me one day, unaware of the fact that I was actually eating the last of three.

I listened with growing despair as other people spoke of overeating—which in *their* eyes meant consuming a second helping of potatoes or an extra sliver of pie. For me, overeating was something altogether different. It meant consuming whatever there was until there wasn't any more. I would only stop eating once the cookie box was empty, once the candy dish was clean, once the last of whatever it happened to be was gone.

Listening to other college students talk about what they had done on spring break, I was suddenly faced with an ugly truth. The only thing I had done, the only thing I could *remember* doing, was devouring huge amounts of cookies. I was appalled to think that this had actually become a major activity in my life, which it had, except for when I was starving myself— or dieting, as I preferred to think of it.

In the early 1970's, there was little talk of eating disorders. The general consensus of opinion was that there were those who knew how to control their appetites and those who did not. Those who did *not* were thought to have very little will power, which was only another way of saying that they were the cause of their own problems.

At that time, I had no way of knowing that I had become ensnared in the early stages of the anorexic-bulimic syndrome. Still, I had begun to realize that there was some sort of cycle involved. Unfortunately, cyclical behavior, particularly in women, is quite commonly accepted as the norm. Depression and mood swings are most often associated with the menstrual cycle, which is blamed for many other things as well.

As for me, I needed nothing else to blame. I blamed myself. I blamed myself even as I continued to do all the things that made me feel guilty and ashamed.

Inevitably, I began to doubt my own ability to make decisions. Decisions about anything at all. By the start of my junior year in college, I was certain I had made the wrong decision by majoring in liberal arts. It seemed to me I should be taking something else. But *what* else? What was I actually suited for? My mother and I discussed it.

"Why don't you major in nutrition?" she suggested. "You've always been interested in cooking and food-oriented things."

It was true, I thought. By learning more about food, I would be able to make more intelligent choices concerning my own diet, and possibly get myself back on the track. A nutrition major sounded like something good to be, and as quickly as that, yet another decision was made. Although it wasn't really *my* decision, it somehow *became* mine through an act of passive acceptance. More often than not, that was my way of handling things.

Unfortunately, it didn't work out as I'd planned. While still in my junior year, I found I could not fit into a dress I had hoped to wear to a cousin's wedding. In desperation, I restricted myself to a diet that consisted of a chunk of cheese and a cracker per day. Of course I lost weight, but after the wedding, I immediately gained it back.

In my senior year, I roomed with two other nutrition majors who firmly believed in perfectly balanced meals. Since they also believed in vigorous exercise, we walked three-and-one-half miles to and from school each day. I was quite willing to adopt their habits in an effort to overcome my own.

By holiday break, I had managed to lose twenty-five pounds. I felt wonderful. I had tons of energy, and eagerly shopped for clothes that were three sizes smaller.

After graduation, I returned home where, as usual, the refrigerator and cupboards were filled to overflowing with snacks and pastries of every kind. That was the kind of home it was. People ate well, enjoyed themselves, and were grateful for what they

15

had. A part of being valued and loved was to allow oneself to be indulged. Within three weeks, I managed to gain back twelve pounds.

Convinced that I had once again been undone by my own lack of self-control, it did not occur to me to look any farther. At that time, I did not even suspect that uncontrollable eating habits might somehow be connected to the repression of negative emotions. I only knew that when food was available, I ate.

I ate, and as I ate, I became increasingly obsessed with the desire for self-control. Control seemed to be the key to everything I wanted in life. At various times I had fought for control in ways I did not even recognize.

While rooming with the two girls who were also nutrition majors, a rather unpleasant situation had occurred. At dinner one night, one of the girls and I were both suddenly determined to sit at the head of the table. Afterwards, we found it impossible to resume our earlier friendship, and no longer spoke to one another.

Many years later I would learn that this incident held far greater significance than I had originally imagined. Had I known what to look for at the time, it would almost certainly have triggered an alarm.

In my determination to sit at the head of the table, I was momentarily seeking *control*. Control— the one thing I had always wanted—control over my life, my fate, and my compulsion to overeat.

16

2

After college, I returned home to Fall River. Although I had not planned to live with my family again, suddenly I was there, wondering what to do with myself. It was a discomforting question for, by then, I had fully expected to have some concrete plans for my life.

I had graduated with about 40 other nutrition majors, at least half of whom were accepted into hospital dietetic internship programs. I, too, had been looking forward to entering such a program in order to complete my education and to become eligible for my registered dietitian's exam. But while my grades were as good as my roommates', they were chosen and I was rejected.

I was deeply disappointed, but not altogether surprised. It seemed to confirm my suspicions that I was somehow lacking. All things being equal, I never quite managed to be as equal as anyone else.

As children, my older sister, Beth, had always been the prettiest. With her thick black braids and huge dimples, she was unmistakably endearing. The word adorable was frequently associated with the things she said and did.

As for Ken, the baby of the family, he was also Mr. Personality. At a remarkably early age, Ken managed to develop an entrepreneur's outlook on life, and once sold the family cat for $20.00. A little later in life, when he started wearing clothes from the men's store my father owned, Ken would often respond to the compliments he received by selling the clothes off his back.

"You like it? You want it? It's yours!" he would say with a grin, and after some swift negotiations, a deal was generally made.

Ken possessed the ability to travel well in any crowd. He was friendly and outgoing, always comfortable and capable of relating well to others. Sensing this, people tended to gravitate toward him.

As for me, I was the child in the middle. I was not as pretty as my sister, not nearly so likable or amusing as my brother. I was simply there—a rather nondescript personality whose looks were average, whose grades in school had always been average, who possessed an average outlook on life.

I went along from one day to the next, waiting for things to happen. To me, life was a kind of preordained storybook. People were born, they grew up, went to school, worked, married, had children, and died. It did not occur to me to question or to deviate from this pattern. Whatever happened to others would eventually happen to me. There was nothing to be done about it, nothing to question or change. In any case, I could think of no way in which to distinguish myself. I possessed no exceptional talents. I had gone to college, and graduated, and nothing was any different. Failing to qualify for the internship program was rather typical of the things I had come to expect out of life. Perhaps it would be best to simply resign myself to what I was, and all the things that I was not.

During this period I received a letter from my brother who was then attending the University of Massachusetts and living on campus. It was an extremely touching letter and I was amazed at its insightfulness.

Ken spoke of how close we were, and how various adversities in life had brought us even closer. He reminded me that I was never alone, that he could readily identify with all of my pain and disappointments.

In an earlier telephone conversation, I had insisted, "You can't possibly know what it's like for me!" but, of course, he did.

"That day was full of tears for me," he had written, referring to the day I had first learned that I would not be accepted into an internship program. "Possibly this is because I recognize your assets more fully than you do."

There were other passages that were similar, that made reference to attributes I found it impossible to identify with. The person he described in his letter was someone he had always admired and looked up to. I could not imagine projecting any quality that was worthy of recognition. Who was this person that others saw? What was expected of her? Obviously she was thought to be happy, vivacious and goal-oriented.

All right! I thought. I would do the things that were expected of me. Whatever else went on in my head—or in my life, it was apparently important to maintain the facade.

Upon hearing that I could become eligible to take the registration exam by earning a master's degree, I signed up to take three graduate level courses at the University of Rhode Island, which necessitated a two-hour drive three or four times per week.

After one week of school, I learned that a local hospital was in need of a nutritionist and immediately applied for the job. I did so at the urging of a boy I was dating at the time, who insisted that practical experience was worth a great deal more than formal education. I was quick to agree. As soon as I learned that I had been accepted for the job, I quit graduate school and went to work.

I was eager to learn all I could about nutrition, and diets, and weight control. Somewhere in all these things I had studied, and was studying still, there had to be a solution to my own problem. How ironic it was that my knowledge and ability to design diets for others had not helped me with my own. I was still an out-of-control eater. If anything, the problem had taken on new dimensions.

By then, I had begun to realize that there was a certain cycle to my eating pattern—a period of control when I was able to dictate what and how much I ate—and a second phase, when I felt I had no control over the amount and types of food I consumed.

Having no clue as to what was causing one cycle to end and another to begin, I felt totally powerless over the shifting moods that contributed to the changes in my eating pattern.

Even so, with an increased knowledge of dieting, energy expenditure, and calorie counting, I learned that there was a balance between how much I ate

20

and how many calories I could burn through metabolism and exercise.

It all began with a small calorie counter that I purchased at the check-out stand of a local supermarket. I took it home and studied it carefully. Soon I had memorized the calorie content of every food listed there — everything from apples to zucchini.

This inevitably led to my next obsession, which concerned itself with keeping daily food diaries. I later expanded these diaries to include all the hours spent in exercising. Everything was carefully monitored and recorded. Each day I pored over my daily successes and failures, feeling either proud or totally devastated by what I saw.

During my binge periods, it was understandably difficult to continue with these diaries, not only because I didn't like what they were telling me, but also because I had little energy or self-discipline. I would find myself fighting the urge to retreat, to go to bed, to sleep around the clock.

Since my weight could easily fluctuate ten to twenty pounds within a single month, my wardrobe soon consisted of three different sizes of clothing. At times, I was overpowered by the unsettling feeling that this was as close as I might ever come to dealing with the problem of my weight.

Through it all, I was constantly preoccupied with the thought of what I would or should eat at my next meal. Food was never out of my mind.

As my eating habits became more bizarre, I developed a highly secretive nature. Whenever I was in anyone's company, I adhered to a model diet, but as soon as I was alone, I would eat whatever was around.

At home, I frequently binged on ice cream, which my mother purchased in half-gallon tubs. Once it was gone, I would go out and buy another tub to replace it. In cases where a tub was only partially full at the time I began my binge, I would see to it that the replacement tub had been eaten down to the same level before returning it to the freezer.

Having become so adept at covering my tracks, I was not prepared for what happened one evening while I was having dinner with friends. The control I had so diligently maintained up until then suddenly abandoned me and I vacuumed up a gargantuan-sized meal. Afterwards, I was appalled to think that I had actually done this in public! It did not occur to me that what I did privately was no less detrimental to my physical and emotional health. The only important thing—or so it seemed—was to keep my problem "under wraps."

For the most part, I just wanted to be alone with food. And yet, whenever I managed to lose, I was thrilled with my new appearance and my heightened energy level. At such times, I would vow never to be heavy again.

"I must never forget what this feels like!" I would say to myself as I whizzed through my day, accomplishing more than most people accomplished in an entire week. "God, it's wonderful to be slim, to feel healthy and attractive again. There's nothing on earth I want more than to feel this way forever!"

And yet, I would eventually want food again. For reasons I could not explain. For reasons I did not even bother to think about. One day, I would simply find myself gorging on potato chips, cashews, ice cream or cookies. By carrying them around in my pockets, it was easy enough for me to consume as many as 60 cookies in a single day.

When two local hospitals, including the one at which I was working, decided to sponsor an internship program, I was chosen as one of three designated interns, and thereafter became involved in a nutritional program that was to be submitted to the American Dietetic Association for approval.

The program was scheduled to run for a period of one year. Each day, I crossed off another number on my calendar, certain in my own mind that once I was actually a registered dietitian, a number of dramatic changes would take place. Surely, by then, I would have the answer I sought! Something I read, something I was taught, or happened to learn through my own research was bound to set me free.

Meanwhile, my sister, who was a teacher, had gotten into the habit of pasting gold stars on my food diary sheets whenever they reflected a day of sensible eating. It was her way of encouraging and supporting me but, of course, it didn't work. In the end, nothing did.

The wonder of it is that I didn't simply give up! Since none of my coping mechanisms had ever really worked, it would have been easy enough to become discouraged. Still, I kept hoping, and trying things, and doing whatever I felt there was left to do in order to get myself back on the track.

Toward the end of my dietetic internship, I decided to reward myself for my professional accomplishments and began to plan a vacation in the Caribbean. My sister, Beth, agreed to accompany me, and since the previous months had gone well in terms of my ability to control my eating, I was looking forward to the trip with much enthusiasm. Even so, I felt the need to shed a few pounds since summer clothes were so revealing. By "bikini time," I hoped to look better than I had ever looked before, which once again caused me to resort to drastic measures.

Lettuce leaves and other low calorie edibles immediately became the mainstay of my diet, and for the first time in my life, I also began to jog. On my initial attempt, I found I was totally winded by the time I had covered a city block, but before long, I was able to run two miles without difficulty. By the time Beth and I were ready to embark upon our trip, I had managed to lose eight pounds.

I had been hoping that something wonderful might happen to me, as people are inclined to do whenever they visit lovely, exotic places. I wanted it to be a special trip, something that would later conjure up special memories—and so it did.

It was while I was vacationing in the Caribbean that I met my husband, Larry.

While he was a quiet, rather studious type of person, I sensed at once that he was not really shy, as others took him to be. He was simply calm and deliberate about things, and possessed an admirably strong and dependable nature. From the outset, I felt totally comfortable with Larry. I enjoyed our conversations together, and also, those long easy periods of silence.

By the end of our trip, my sister, Beth, had lost all interest in the man she was dating, while my interest in Larry had merely intensified.

It was an odd turn of events for, of course, my sister had always been first in everything. And because she was the oldest, it had always been assumed that Beth would be the first to find the right man for her.

Within the family, there was to be much conversation and debate about my relationship with Larry, particularly when I announced my decision to go to New York, where I intended to live with him until he had finished medical school.

"And what are his intentions?" my mother immediately asked, as mothers are inclined to do.

I said I didn't know, that it was too early to tell.

"How can it be too early?" she countered. "You've got to think about your future in a situation like this."

I tried to explain that I wasn't getting myself into any situation, but then again, who could really be sure? Although I had extremely high hopes for Larry and me, I wasn't altogether unrealistic. I knew that our life in New York would not be an endless romance. It would expose us to the everydayness of things, and make it impossible for us to keep presenting our "best sides" to one another.

Although I was not particularly concerned about any negative qualities that Larry might reveal to me, I was concerned about certain character flaws in myself, and how Larry would ultimately be affected by them. While I wanted to be a good wife to him—if and when it came to that—I had no real perception of what actually constituted such a person—or even what sort of wife Larry might prefer to have. I knew he would need a lot of time to himself, and that his studies would take precedence over everything else. Perhaps the best thing would be to stay out of his hair, and to become as self-sufficient as I possibly could.

25

In retrospect, it is interesting to reflect upon my conflicting philosophies of life at this particular time, for while I fully intended to stand on my own two feet, I was also looking at Larry as a possible "cure" for all my problems. It is impossible to say exactly how I hoped he might help me to overcome my bouts with binge eating since he was not even aware of them. And in keeping with the behavior patterns I had always followed in the past, I was determined to keep my problem hidden. Even so, I had no difficulty convincing myself that Larry was the answer to everything. And that living in New York would provide me with a totally new environment in which to "heal myself."

I was not altogether prepared for life in a medical school housing facility—where cooking was done in a communal kitchen, and where the atmosphere was unmistakably "institutional." We lived on the corner of 98th Street and Fifth Avenue, across from Central Park.

For the first few months, I occupied myself by walking up and down the streets each day, looking into shop windows and patronizing a nearby bakery. The bakery sold wonderfully hot, aromatic loaves of French bread which I loved to eat after smearing them with huge slabs of butter.

One day, as I sat in our small apartment, munching away, I realized I would have to find a job in order to break through this latest cycle of gorging myself.

And so I went to work at Gimbel's Department Store, selling pots and pans during the holiday season. But once the holidays had passed, I was im-

26

mediately laid off, and so I began going to registered dietitian's meetings. Because of a contact I happened to make there, I was eventually hired by the Veteran's Administration Hospital.

Having taken and passed my registration exam, I went to work for the VA as a clinical dietitian in the South Bronx. I was delighted to have found this opening since I saw it as a means of launching my own career.

Meanwhile, Larry and I lived together and managed to get along as well as couples are inclined to do in the earliest phases of a relationship. There were the inevitable adjustments to be made.

One Sunday morning, I fixed a special breakfast in our communal kitchen, only to have Larry tell me, once it was ready, that he wanted to watch the rest of a television interview.

Unable to deal with this objectively, I began to internalize, and ultimately concluded that Larry did not really care for me, or my cooking, that I never managed to do anything right, and that I probably never would.

There were days when just our living accommodations were enough to depress me, for we lived on the eighth floor of an old nursing dorm building, and shared bathroom facilities with other people, most of whom were men.

Before I came to New York, Larry had lived alone on the ninth floor of this facility, and through my communications with him, the number 920 had become firmly ingrained in my mind. Because of this, an unfortunate mix-up occurred one cold and rainy evening when we decided to have some pizzas delivered. I inadvertently gave out the wrong room number and, as a consequence, our food never arrived.

Eventually, I realized my mistake and confessed to Larry what I had done.

"My God," he said, totally infuriated now, "how could you do such a stupid thing? Our room number is 840, not 920. Don't you even know where you live?"

Assuming he would find the incident as comical as I had, I was somewhat taken aback by his sudden anger. Afterwards, being too stupid to remember my own address was the only remark of his that permanently stuck in my mind.

Although I was quick to accept myself as totally inept, there was no denying that I had become an expert in at least one area of my life. In analyzing anyone's personal opinions or feelings about me, I was extremely skilled at picking out only the negative references (either real or imagined), which I immediately magnified to a degree that was truly alarming! It would leave me with a feeling of total worthlessness, and the attending fear that I would always be forced to find my identity through someone else.

If Larry eventually married me, I would then be a doctor's wife. That was a commendable thing to be, and a status in life definitely worth attaining.

As if to support this view, I began receiving letters and phone calls from home. Well-intentioned people who loved me reminded me that I wasn't getting any younger, that I wasn't the brightest or prettiest girl in the world, and that Larry might well be my one and only chance for wedded bliss. I was further reminded that a state of co-habitation was a risky business at best, that uncommitted men were known to walk out on the women they professed to love, and that this might easily happen to me.

I grew extremely anxious at the thought, and finally asked Larry for a commitment. Knowing it might well lead to a heated argument between us, I was relieved when he reacted in a totally calm and reasonable way.

Larry explained that he wanted to be sure about us, that he didn't want to make a mistake on so large an issue as this.

"I've made some impulsive decisions in my life that I later regretted," he said. "I want us both to be happy, Dorie. That's the only reason I've been cautious. It has nothing to do with not loving you for, of course, I do."

In the way he stated his argument, I had no choice but to believe him. In all matters of importance, I knew I could always count on him to be level-headed and fair—and kind.

And so I laid the matter to rest, returning once again to my earlier view that whatever became of us was undoubtedly inevitable. Regardless of anything else that could be said for such a position, I instinctively knew that it had logic and maturity on its side.

3

Larry graduated from medical school with an impressive scholastic record, which came as no surprise to anyone. He was extremely smart, and also, a perfectionist. Most of his college education, including four years of medical school, had been scholastically funded.

In July 1978, we moved to Cleveland, where Larry undertook his internship and residency.

As for me, I once again became affiliated with the Veteran's Administration Hospital, where I assumed another clinical dietitian's position. The clinic where Larry was working was approximately three miles away.

A small problem that quickly became a major one concerned itself with the fact that we only had one car. Since Larry began work at 7:00 a.m., I would drive him to the clinic at an hour that seemed to arrive a bit earlier every day. And once the day had ended, which, for me, was generally around 4:00, I would need to pick up Larry, who was occasionally done at 5:00, but whose shift could also run as late as 8:00 or 9:00 p.m.

It soon became a life of "waiting for Larry," or so it seemed when I was the most irritable and depressed. I would drive home each afternoon, knowing that I would need to go out again, and that dinner was something I would be eating alone. Of course, it was easier to gorge myself when Larry was not there, and I frequently did so, then later blamed him, totally ignoring the fact that this was a habit I had acquired long before meeting Larry.

My mood swings became more frequent, and increasingly severe. One day I would be extremely happy, and the next, so despondent that I could barely drive a car. I would often find myself sitting at a traffic light with tears streaming down my face. Had anyone asked me to explain the reason for my overwhelming despair, I could not possibly have done so. Life was simply more than I could bear.

I had expected to be happy in Cleveland, just as I had expected to be happy with Larry. I began to wonder if I would be happier if we were married. Perhaps I was not meant for a casual, live-in relationship. There was no denying that I had been raised to believe in the sanctity of marriage. I began to suspect that I was unconsciously troubled by our immediate arrangement and that I could not be happy until Larry and I were totally committed to one another.

At that time, I could not possibly have known that this particular pattern of thought was actually a chronic part of my problem. To always place my happiness outside myself—to continue to insist that it would come through some particular event or person, accomplished nothing except to perpetuate the lie. And, of course, it did nothing to resolve my immediate frustrations.

I took a certain amount of pride in controlling my anger, which would fester until it suddenly

31

erupted with alarming force. At such times, Larry would be totally unprepared for everything that followed, particularly in the case of the car.

One night, when he came out of the clinic, I immediately began screaming at him.

Once he understood that this tirade had something to do with all the time I spent waiting to pick him up, Larry agreed that we should buy a second car. I was immediately pacified, believing, once again, that every problem in my life would be resolved once this purchase was actually made.

Despite the demands upon his time, it is to Larry's credit that he attempted to do all he could to make me happy. Sensing that I needed to have him spend more time with me, he agreed to accompany me on a shopping trip.

By the time we had visited several stores, I had become nervous and irritable with what I perceived to be Larry's impatience or boredom.

"This is all just a waste of time!" I finally snapped. "I shouldn't have asked you to come along."

Larry was understandably bewildered by my sudden mood change but, by then, he had grown accustomed to them. When I suggested we return home, he merely shrugged and nodded, assuming perhaps that I had had enough shopping for one day.

That proves it! I thought, as we walked back to the car. He was just waiting for a reason to get out of this!

At work, I had made the acquaintance of two women who would eventually become my best friends. During coffee and lunch breaks, we often sat together, consuming Pepperidge Farm cookies which were conveniently packaged in three separate layers.

As each of us consumed a layer of cookies, we confided in one another on both a personal and professional level. I was always careful to avoid the major issue of my life which, of course, concerned itself with my compulsive eating habits. In the company of others, I was still simulating normal behavior, and since the other girls were "munching" too, my own love affair with food was not particularly conspicuous.

But as food began to dominate my life, my friendships began to deteriorate. In one instance, I was even forced to cancel a dinner date with one friend who had intended to take me out on my birthday. By evening of that particular day, I had already eaten so much that I knew I could never consume another meal. I was steeped in guilt and remorse when this friend nonetheless had flowers delivered to me.

That night, since Larry was working late, I went to bed early and quickly escaped into sleep. This was something I had begun to do more frequently now in an effort to avoid my problems.

Whenever I found it impossible to sleep, I would reflect upon the various incidents of that day, trying to determine exactly where I had gone wrong, and how I might have managed things better.

Learning how to properly balance a checkbook was something I vowed to do once Larry and I had argued about it.

"It's such a simple thing!" he had insisted one evening in a state of total exasperation. Unable to understand my inability to accurately add and subtract, he resorted instead to instilling within me a fear of an embarrassing overdraft.

"It's bound to happen, you know, if you never have any idea how much money you've got in the account."

"But I do know!" I insisted. "Even if it isn't reconciled right to the penny, I do have a reasonable idea."

"What about the monthly charges that the bank automatically deducts? Service charges—charges for imprinting checks. If you've already made a mistake, those additional charges could be just enough to overdraw the account. No, Dorie, you can't just keep assuming about this. If you're going to do it, then at least do it right."

Larry, the perfectionist! I found myself thinking. Whatever I did, he would always be able to do it better.

As my confidence and self-esteem continued to deteriorate, life became increasingly difficult. Even so, I was determined to improve—to be as perfect as it was possible to be.

I decided to concentrate on those things I knew how to do well. I cooked delicious and attractive meals, thinking of them as 'little celebrations,' for there was generally an occasion involved. The occasion was often a minor thing, minor or even inconsequential, so that Larry's indifference was only to be expected. Even so, I would wait to be told how lovely everything was—what a delicious surprise—and hadn't I been wonderful to think of it?

But Larry was a basically non-reactive person. Whatever he enjoyed, he enjoyed quietly. Knowing this, I nonetheless expected him to step totally out of character and respond in the way that I wanted him to. He didn't, of course, and so, I felt crushed and defeated.

Rarely, if ever, did I concentrate on Larry's attributes—all those wonderful qualities that had attracted me to him in the first place.

On days when I was in a positive frame of mind, we shared a special closeness, and were truly happy together. Larry could be a clown, and frequently had me laughing so hard that my sides ached. These were the times when I knew—really knew—that he and I were meant for one another. I could not imagine being with anyone else; he was the only one I wished to share my life with.

The tragedy in all this is that I never felt secure in my relationship with Larry, for I did not really believe myself worthy of such a person. And, as if to reinforce my fears, something would always happen that would once again cause him to become cross with me.

On one occasion, we had agreed to meet at a Chinese restaurant for dinner. Since there were two such places that we frequently patronized, Larry went to one while I went to the other. After we had both waited around for a while, we climbed back into our cars and drove off in the opposite direction, passing one another en route. We did this three or four times, and then finally both drove home, where I assumed we would decide, once and for all, where we were going, and then go there. The entire thing was such a comedy of errors that I found myself laughing out loud—but only until I realized that Larry was not amused. After an extremely demanding day, he had no energy or patience for this sort of Keystone Kops scenario, and shouted and carried on in a manner that would have been far more typical of me.

As always, I was left with the feeling that I would never manage to do things right—that nothing about me was right, and that Larry deserved someone better.

In March of 1979, Larry and I were married.

The wedding was held in Fall River where my parents lived, and in view of this, my family handled all the arrangements. Nothing was required of Larry and me except to show up at the appointed time, and while we managed to do this, my parents, who met us at the airport, were shocked to discover that we were not speaking to each other.

My brother had arranged a little party which we attended but took no active part in. Seating ourselves at opposite ends of the room, we simply glowered and sulked.

Although I had very much wanted to be married, I no longer knew if we were doing the right thing. Still, we were here. Why had we come, if not to go through with this?

That weekend, we were married in a small but beautiful ceremony. Once it was over, I felt happy and confident again. Petty little arguments notwithstanding, Larry and I were still the ideal couple. The real problem—as I saw it—concerned itself with becoming the ideal wife.

I sincerely believed that happily married people were those who never argued. They never argued—and somehow, just being married seemed to solve everything else for them as well.

Although I had never personally known of such a marriage, I had read of such things in novels, and observed a number of stereotypical couples on TV. They were always pleasant and romantically inclined toward one another. The bloom was never off the rose. The magic and excitement were always there.

As I expectantly waited to share in all this, the routine of our days continued along as before. Soon I was forced to admit that nothing in my life with Larry had really changed. Our living arrangement was legal now, but beyond that, everything was exactly the same.

Feeling a trifle disillusioned with things, I wrote out a long list of complaints which I later discussed with Larry. I was surprised to hear him agree with much of what I had to say. He promised to try harder—to do better, to devote more time and attention to us—to more evenly balance out his life between work and home.

At this stage in Larry's life, it was easier said than done. Over a period of time, I saw only slight and sporadic improvement. Unable to identify with his professional ambitions, I went to my own job each day and gave it the customary amount of time required. It was not something that made any great demands upon me, nor was it something I intended to devote the rest of my life to.

Actually, I had no real concept of what I wanted to do professionally. At times, I was filled with incredible energy and enthusiasm—ready to take on the world—but there was also the darker, moodier side of my nature that frequently made it impossible for me to function.

As time went on, I gradually came to a frightening realization. My moods, as I had always referred to them, were becoming so mentally and physically debilitating that they could now be accurately categorized as severe depression.

The term itself had never meant a great deal to me.

There are, of course, various stages and categories of depression, including one which is actually "anger turned inward." A person who has been programmed not to express anger, who affords himself no means of airing his frustrations, will often become a victim of severe depression.

At the time of my marriage, I had not yet realized that emotions—good or bad—are simply realities of life. It seemed to me that every effort needed to be made to maintain the "status quo." My anger and petty resentments over such things as having only one car to drive were repressed for as long as possible, resulting in the inevitable "explosion."

Although I always later regretted my uncontrollable outbursts, I was never astute enough to change the pattern of behavior that inevitably led up to them.

Nor did I see any relationship between my binge eating and my inability to express anger.

Another form of depression that had begun to plague me was the depression associated with guilt. Had anyone thought to ask me what I felt guilty about, the answer might well have been "Everything!"

Because I was the product of so many incorrect decisions and beliefs about myself, guilt had become a constant companion.

As a child, I had always regarded myself as the nondescript middle child—the one no one noticed because of an older, prettier sister, and a younger, personality-plus brother.

As a young adult, I had begun to identify through "my husband, the doctor," someone whose love and respect seemed at risk whenever we engaged in an argument. I had no way of knowing that, for Larry, an argument was merely an isolated incident, and that it did not affect his basic feelings for me.

Had I been able to talk honestly with him, to express my inner fears and doubts, these anxieties might easily have been laid to rest. But I did not know how to talk to Larry, and even had I known, I would not have known what to ask him for.

While working at the VA Hospital, I gradually became a vending machine addict. I always carried a great deal of change with me with which I purchased my daily "stash" of candy, cookies, peanuts and chewing gum.

A nearby bakery frequently tempted me with its fresh and sugary delights. It was not uncommon for me to go there and purchase six doughnuts and four giant-sized cookies which I could easily consume in a space of one or two hours. Afterwards, I always felt extremely nauseated but this did not keep me from making additional purchases on my way home—two pints of ice cream, a large bag of potato chips, a can of cashews, or some packages of M & M's—whatever I felt was needed to carry me through the evening.

At the end of such a binge, I was often too sick to function, and this feeling would last for a period of several days.

At such times, I lost all interest in personal hygiene since showering or bathing was something that forced me to look at my own body. I slept a great deal of the time, or if I was awake, I was generally immersed in an impenetrable cloud of self-loathing.

My frequent withdrawals from life eventually became a source of concern to others. In one case, I accidentally knocked the telephone receiver off its hook, which made it impossible for a friend to call me. After trying to reach me all day, she finally called the guardhouse at the entrance to our building.

The guard came to our apartment and repeatedly knocked on the door. Although I was home, I was not in the mood to see anyone, and so, I did not answer. Nor did I answer when the knocking turned into pounding. I kept waiting for whoever it was to go away. Finally, I heard a key in the lock, and a few moments later, the security guard walked in.

Once he explained that my friend had been trying to reach me all day, I walked over to the phone and quickly replaced the receiver. After that, I awkwardly stood about as the guard apologized for disturbing me.

"Oh no—that's all right," I told him. "I guess I must've fallen asleep."

"Well, it's just that things happen sometimes—you never know if someone's fallen and broken a leg. Or if they've slipped in the shower and—"

"Yes, yes—I know."

Sensing my embarrassment and impatience, the guard eventually left. Afterwards, I was angry—angry at having been intruded upon, angry at my friend for having called the guard—angry at having been momentarily forced out of my lethargy.

The real cause for my anger, of course, was that it forced me back into reality. Back into a world of problems that I could not seem to solve.

Once the door had closed behind the security guard, I sat down and thought about what I should do.

What was actually involved in solving a problem?

Whenever a person found himself in a situation in which he was motivated to achieve a certain goal, but in which his progress was blocked by some obstacle, he was confronted with a problem.

The solution to the problem involved the development of some mode of response that would eliminate the obstacle.

That was it. Pure and simple.

Once I had known what to do about things. Hadn't I? Hadn't I once been able to evaluate a situation, to sift through the various options available to me, to objectively arrive at the best possible solution?

It was difficult to remember. For what seemed like a very long time now, my thinking had been so terribly muddled! Even now, I could not decide if I should stay up or go back to bed. I did not know what I should fix for dinner that night, whether I should continue to hold onto a job that no longer challenged me, whether or not I should go on a diet, and if so, which one?

I felt suddenly panicky—panicky in a way that made it difficult to breathe. Perhaps I was losing my mind! After all, there was no rational cause for most of my behavior and thought patterns. The anxieties and frustrations I felt. The ideas I had about myself and others. My fear of losing Larry. My compulsive

41

eating. My inability to cope. And now, this tendency to hide away. What was it all leading to?

I glanced at the clock and saw that it was getting late. If Larry came home on time, he would be here soon. With that realization came the immediate thought that I must conceal whatever was wrong. As usual, it seemed more important to appear all right than to actually be all right.

But as I scurried around, straightening the apartment, preparing something for us to eat, I sensed that the answer was not to be found in this constant habit of role-playing. On the other hand, I did not dare to be myself. If Larry knew what I actually did all day, if he had any idea how much I ate, how much I hated myself, how anxious and afraid of everything I was, what would become of us?

One day he called the VA Hospital and asked to speak with me only to learn I had not come in because I was sick. That evening, he asked me about it.

"What's wrong?" he wanted to know. "You seem fine to me."

After I had given him a lot of vague answers, I finally admitted that I hadn't gone in because I simply hadn't felt up to it.

"Well, either you're sick or you're not sick," he persisted.

"Oh Larry, it isn't that. It's just that I'm so fat!"

Larry looked at me and laughed, but totally without humor.

"What kind of reason is that for not going to work, Dorie? People depend on you to do the job you were hired for. Being too fat has nothing to do with anything. Just eat less and that problem will solve itself."

"It isn't that simple!" I told him, whereupon he immediately insisted it was.

We argued a while longer and, as usual, nothing was actually resolved. But one thing that was firmly established was that I was acting irresponsibly in refusing to go to work.

It was true! I thought. I was irresponsible—in addition to everything else I was. I tried to think of something I could write down on the asset side of the ledger—anything at all—but even after I had thought about it long and hard, absolutely nothing came to mind.

4

By the end of 1982, I had begun to engage in a totally non-functional ritual which soon had all the dietetic staff members at the VA Hospital talking about me. As the hospital's nutrition clinic dietitian, I worked with out-patients, and next to my desk was a scale on which I began to weigh myself as often as ten or fifteen times each day. Although the reading never reflected the dramatic weight loss I was hoping for, I persisted in getting on and off the scale until a supervisor finally asked me about it.

Had she been a trifle more insightful, she might have been able to recognize this form of compulsive behavior as evidence of some deeper problem, but as it was, she merely asked if it was necessary for me to weigh myself that often, which, I suppose, was her way of encouraging me to stop.

In the end, she helped me to decide that it was time to quit my job. By then, I no longer had any interest in my work, and the ordeal of driving back and forth each day was becoming more than I could bear.

Since my work was the one thing that had provided some structure to my life, I could ill-afford to be without it. Even so, I did quit my job, and afterwards—from December 1982 to June of 1983, I spent most of my life in bed.

Around Christmastime, my favorite ice cream parlor temporarily closed down, which was as distressing to me as a death in the family might have been to someone else. When it reopened, I was their first customer, and so, life continued along.

I behaved as normally as I could around Larry, preparing nice dinners, and listening to him whenever he wanted to talk. On those nights when he didn't want to talk, I assumed he was angry with me, although he was usually just tired.

He was, however, displeased with my decision to quit working, for he sensed that I needed something to do. Then too, it made absolutely no sense to squander away my time, wasting a good education and the opportunity to utilize it in some positive way.

But, by then, I had lost all faith in my ability to perform any constructive function. I could barely manage to carry on a conversation with friends who occasionally called to invite me out to lunch. Although I would promise to get back to them, somehow I never did, and after a while, my friends simply quit calling.

One particular friend, who was also a dietitian, was understandably confused by my dysfunctional behavior in view of the fact that we had intended to go into business together. The plan was to start up a weight loss class that we would open to the public once we had found a suitable location and had done a little advertising.

Although we agreed to equally divide all the preliminary work involved, I never quite managed to get my end of things done. When my friend would ask if I had seen the printers that day, or if I had arranged an appointment with people who had a meeting room available, I was always forced to say no.

The fact was, I had already reached a point where it was becoming difficult for me to perform even simple errands. Taking a letter to the post office for Larry was something I really had to struggle with, and it did not always get done. In view of this, it seemed best to make no commitments, to totally avoid people, and to simply let them drift away.

At this particular time, I was only vaguely aware that Larry was wrestling with problems of his own. For several months, he had been investigating various job offers, all of which were located in remote little towns that provided virtually no opportunity for advancement. After twenty-five years of formal schooling, Larry could see no way of earning anything that even resembled an adequate income. As time passed, he grew increasingly discouraged, and ever more impatient with my own unwillingness to work, since jobs were more readily available to me. But I found it impossible to motivate myself. Even the fact that we needed the extra income was not enough to bring me out of my lethargic state.

Lethargy and depression were all I had known for a very long time when Larry suddenly received a job offer in Phoenix, Arizona. It came from a group of established gastroenterologists who had once gone through the same Cleveland Clinic program that Larry had gone through.

During the interview, he was disappointed to hear them say that they hadn't yet firmly decided whether or not to take on another doctor.

"Don't let us hold you up," they said, obviously assuming that Larry had a number of other positions to consider.

We returned to Cleveland, and there in the mail was a contract offer from Pittsburgh, Pennsylvania—a mediocre offer at best, and in an area where we did not particularly care to live.

Suddenly, Larry was depressed—as depressed as I had ever known him to be. It hadn't occurred to me how much I had come to rely upon his calm, even-tempered demeanor until it was no longer there for me to fall back on. I became dreadfully concerned about him—concerned about us both, for it seemed that we had lost all ability to communicate, that our marriage was floundering, and perhaps, would not even survive.

Once this thought occurred to me, I recognized it as a familiar one. Unconsciously, I had been thinking about this for some time. Larry and I no longer together. Larry on his own—far better off without me. As for me, I could not envision anything beyond our breakup. I did not see myself in any particular place, doing anything of consequence—or even anything at all. It was as if I would simply cease to exist once Larry and I were divorced.

When the job offer in Phoenix at last came through—something Larry had very nearly given up on by the time it actually happened—I briefly shared his elation, but then sank back into my depression.

"Maybe I shouldn't go with you," I said to him one day. "It might be best if we just end it right here."

Accepting this as another of my moods, Larry did his best to work around it. There was a great deal to

47

do, and as we started packing, my spirits gradually improved, and I became a little more optimistic.

I began to think of life in a warm, sunny climate. There, I would not be able to hide my excess weight under layers and layers of winter clothing. I would need to slim down so that I would look good in sportswear and swimsuits. I would be jogging a lot, getting a tan, eating fresh citrus off the trees—doing a lot of things that were good for me. Yes, life would be better there, and I would be better as well. I couldn't really help but be.

We made the move in the month of July, and since Larry did not have to begin work until August 1, we devoted ourselves to setting up our new apartment. The time we spent together was extremely productive, and I remember how happy and almost well I felt. I was confident that this, at last, was to be the major turning point in my life.

Meeting Larry hadn't quite been it.

Nor had becoming a registered dietitian.

Even getting married hadn't quite done the trick.

But now, this would be it! I was certain of it, as certain as I had ever been of anything in my entire life.

But then Larry went to work, and suddenly, I was alone. It occurred to me then that I did not know a single soul in the entire city. I had no job, no friends, no connection with anything or anyone.

Each day, I would find myself waiting for Larry to come home, but when he did, he was not all that interesting or amusing to be around.

At the Cleveland Clinic, he had been involved in a teaching program that kept him extremely busy. But now, in the early stages of building his own practice, he found himself with a great deal of time on his hands. Unaccustomed to this, he was often preoccupied, which left me feeling more isolated than ever.

I began jogging in the mornings, and would frequently pass a pregnant woman who was walking in the opposite direction. One day I stopped and introduced myself, and after that, I thought of this woman as my "only friend," although I knew nothing at all about her, not even her last name.

It was while I was jogging that it suddenly occurred to me that I should probably see a psychiatrist. Perhaps something had happened in my childhood that was responsible for the way I was now, for the fact that I could not seem to get a grip on life. But a psychiatrist was a luxury—and what if he didn't find anything wrong?

On the heels of this sobering thought, I returned home and went back to bed, where I remained until it was time to order lunch. It was necessary to order it since there was never any great amount of food in the house. I felt better—safer—surrounded by empty cupboards, although this never kept me from ordering huge take-out pizzas, or anything else I might suddenly have developed a craving for.

As I quickly regained the weight I had lost before leaving Cleveland, I grew increasingly disgusted with myself, and also, increasingly depressed.

Depression was now a constant, pervasive thing. Had anyone asked, I would have described my life in totally negative terms. I could no longer conceive of things getting any better. Even so, I still believed in brief respites from depression—even counted on them to occur. Each time they did, I would race around and accomplish as much as I possibly could before another inevitable cloud of gloom-and-doom descended upon me.

Looking back into the past, I could remember only the bad things that had happened to me. Looking ahead, I could see nothing but a snarl of never-ending problems. Beyond that, there was only emptiness.

Whatever I was actually saying or doing at this time was apparently disturbing enough to get Larry's attention, for he became extremely concerned about me. In time, he would even suggest that I seek out professional help. It distressed me to hear him say this, for I had always taken great pride in my ability to act "normal" around him, no matter how bad things actually were. I decided that I must be "slipping fast" if I had begun to betray myself, and obviously I had, for soon, my parents were as concerned about me as my husband.

And then, one day, my sister arrived for a visit. She came shortly after my mother and I had talked long distance on the phone. I knew she had been sent as a kind of advance scout since that had always been my family's way of doing things. Then too, my sister's husband was a psychiatrist. Undoubtedly, the family had had some interesting discussions about me, and quite possibly, had arrived at some alarming conclusions.

One of the things that had certainly alarmed Larry was something that occurred one evening while he and I were fixing dinner together. At some point, I simply picked up my sunglasses and walked out the door. Although I had no idea where I was going, I had absolutely no intention of ever coming back.

Some distance from home, I sat down on the curb and started to cry. A short while later, Larry appeared and asked what I was doing there.

"I'm running away," I told him, much as a child might have said it.

"Come on—let's go home," Larry immediately responded.

"No!" I told him. "I don't ever want to go back there again. It isn't any use, Larry. I just can't go on the way I am. It isn't fair to you."

"Dorie, what are you talking about? What is all this? One minute, I was standing in the kitchen talking to you, and the next minute, I turned around and you were gone. Why didn't you tell me you were leaving?"

"Because I'm running away from home! You don't tell people when you're running away from home. You just do it!"

For one long moment, Larry simply stared at me, trying to make some sense out of things.

"All right," he finally said. "Running away isn't the answer. You know that as well as I do."

"Then what is the answer?" I asked, once again very close to tears.

"Let's go back to the house and talk about it," he suggested, and after a while, that was exactly what we did.

After we had mutually agreed that some form of therapy was necessary, I looked through the yellow pages of the phone book, then wrote down the name of a doctor. The only reason I selected him is because he happened to have the same last name as the high school I had once attended. For some unexplainable reason, I saw this as a positive sign.

Once the appointment had been made, I immediately had second thoughts. I found myself worrying about the questions I would be asked, wondering if I could answer them in a way that would manage to create a favorable impression.

I wanted to appear reasonably well-adjusted, and totally functional in terms of having some purpose in this world. Perhaps I could talk about my job.

By then, I had gone to work at a local gourmet shop that specialized in such items as imported cheeses, wines, and fine French breads. Not surprisingly, I had become a perpetual "muncher" as I worked around these foods, so that each eight-hour shift soon escalated into a veritable eating bonanza. Although there were days when I managed to have some control over my eating, there were other days when I ate everything in sight. As a consequence, I continued to experience tremendous fluctuations in my weight and in my moods.

How would I ever manage to explain this life of extremes to a total stranger? Would he be repulsed by the fact that I could easily consume in excess of 5,000 calories in a day, that I could eat until my stomach was totally distended, until the food was beginning to back up into my throat? What would he think of someone who could make themselves so sick from eating that they were literally incapacitated for several days afterward? I could not imagine myself engaging in such embarrassing confessions, and yet I would have to. Wouldn't I?

Not knowing what to expect, I was hardly prepared for what actually occurred. In my initial interview with this doctor, I was surprised to hear him say that he believed I might have a learning disorder.

"Most people I see have learning disorders," he said, in a way that made me feel he had come to some sort of generalized conclusion about all of us.

"Another thing," he said, "I notice that your ears don't quite match, and the tips of your little fingers curve downward ever so slightly."

As I sat there wondering what this could possibly mean, I heard him suggest that I undergo a hearing test.

After I had tentatively agreed to be tested, I left this doctor's office, and never again returned.

For the next several days, I felt much better—perhaps because I had made the decision to stop seeing this particular doctor, or because it was simply time for me to feel better again.

The fact was, the changes in my moods seemed totally unrelated to anything that was happening in my life. Nor did they appear to be related to any biological changes that regularly occurred. Try as I might, I could never blame my moods on anything that might have given me a logical reason for feeling angry, frustrated or depressed.

I began to wonder if it was simply a case of mind over matter. If I could somehow bring myself to concentrate on having a good attitude, it might help me to cope and to eventually work out my problems.

As resolutions go, it was as good as any I had ever made—and worked out about as well. As my good mood gradually deteriorated into another bad one, I found it impossible to hold onto any form of positive thinking, and soon, I was once again depressed.

By now, I had noticed that each period of depression was becoming longer and far more intense. It was a frightening realization, causing me to wonder if I was actually going insane!

Here was a thought that was simply too dreadful to contemplate. No, I immediately decided, it couldn't possibly be that! More than likely, I was just a little neurotic, a little overly anxious about things.

Whatever I was, I knew beyond any doubt that I was no longer well. And it wasn't enough to say I was a moody person. Not anymore.

On impulse, I quit my job at the gourmet shop, doing it abruptly, without giving any prior notice. Although my employer was extremely upset with me, I no longer cared. I knew I could not afford to stay there and, on a daily basis, continue to eat an entire loaf of bread, a pound of cheese—whatever happened to be around. And so I quit, and ran.

After that, I sank into yet another deep depression, as black and ominous a mood as I had ever experienced. My only thought, as I struggled to come out of it, was that I must force myself to take some positive action! Given another chance, I vowed I would DO something about myself. Whatever it took. Whatever it cost. I would do it! And so, I prayed for that second chance—prayed for it in earnest, for I strongly suspected that it might already be too late.

5

On January 2, 1984, I began my therapy session with another doctor, a psychoanalyst this time. During the next eighteen months, we reviewed every aspect of my childhood and family life, and meanwhile, my moods continued to fluctuate.

In the month of April, I went to work for CIGNA Healthplan of Arizona and, once again, had high hopes that this might be the thing that would finally turn my life around.

By then, I was taking anti-depressant medication, a method of treatment I had little if any faith in. The side effects included dryness of the mouth, constipation, and a weird variety of aches and pains. Worst of all was my own suspicion that I was merely masking my problems rather than curing them.

One day I simply stopped taking my pills, and after that, I felt great! Among other things, I found I had suddenly developed an ability to control my appetite. For the first time in years, I was able to recognize when I was full, and encountered no difficulty in leaving a little food on my plate.

While I was altogether thrilled with the thought that I might actually be cured, my joy was short-lived, for I soon began binging again.

At this juncture, I began to undergo some serious analysis, and actually laid on a couch twice a week while the doctor and I delved ever deeper into my psyche.

While I managed to gain certain insights, we never quite touched on what I was actually feeling, perhaps because I did not know, or was not yet ready to know. In any event, my fluctuating moods and uncontrollable eating habits continued. Finally, I agreed to go back on medication.

This time, I was given a drug that threw me into a perpetual state of hypermania. I found it impossible to sleep for more than three hours each night, and rarely consumed more than 500 calories in a day.

In a matter of ten weeks, my weight had dropped to 92 pounds, and I was immediately urged to go off my medication.

"I will—in just a few more days," I promised my doctor, determined to give myself a little "cushion" in case I started gaining again.

One day in November, I fell while I was jogging, and while the injury to my leg was only minor, it somehow never quite managed to heal. After a month, it was still an open wound, which made me realize that the nutrients in my body were not sufficient to promote any healing. At that, I became truly alarmed!

At the time of my next weigh-in, I was suddenly faced with an ultimatum.

"Unless you manage to gain some weight—at least two pounds over the weekend," my doctor insisted, "I'll have no choice but to put you in the hospital."

And so, I stopped taking my pills. Although I was determined to watch my weight, to remain as sleek and firm as I was, before very long, I had managed to gain ten pounds. Another ten was quickly added to that, and soon, I was 30 pounds heavier.

With this came the usual cloud of depression, which caused the doctor to assume that I might actually be manic-depressive. In an effort to correct the chemical imbalance that was thought to be causing this, some Lithium was prescribed for me, which accomplished nothing except to aggravate my moods, and to cause excessive bloating.

Once I had been taken off Lithium, I struggled along for another five months, and finally, my doctor suggested that I see a psychopharmacologist, someone who had a specialized knowledge of drugs, their preparation, qualities and uses.

While this appointment was being arranged for me, I sat quietly and stared at the floor. I had begun to suspect that there was no viable answer for me. After all, so much had already been tried, including everything that I had tried on my own.

What was this unclassified eating disorder? Somehow it did not seem to fall into the category of either anorexia or bulimia. Although I was bulimic to the extent that I frequently engaged in eating binges, I did not take laxatives, or force myself to vomit up what I had eaten. On the anorexia side, I only occasionally got around to starving myself, and never for prolonged periods of time.

Whatever was wrong with me was something no one seemed to have a label for. Even manic-depression did not really describe it.

My full-time job at CIGNA, while adding some structure and purpose to my life, had not provided any miraculous cure. In fact, as time went on, I frequently called in sick and then spent the balance of the day in bed, until it was time for Larry to come home. By the time he arrived, I would be showered and dressed, and ready to serve him his dinner.

Another typical day in the life of a typical housewife—except that I was becoming increasingly irritable and intolerant of everyday situations.

At times, I would burst into hysterical rages over inconsequential matters, perhaps because I was living in a chronically defensive state.

Knowing that Larry would inevitably learn of my absences from work was cause for constant concern. There seemed to be nothing I could do to alter my pattern of behavior, although I very much wanted to, if only to keep from getting caught.

"I called the office today and they said you had called in sick," Larry remarked one evening, as I had known he would. Even as he said it, he looked at me suspiciously, for we had already been through this many times.

There was nothing I could say in my own defense, except what I had said before. That I was too fat! That I simply couldn't face up to working that day.

It resulted in the inevitable argument between us, with Larry insisting once again that people were paying me to work, not to lie around in bed.

I knew this only too well, for it was part of the thing that was constantly chipping away at me.

In an effort to feel good about myself, it had always been necessary to adopt another coping mechanism. The problem was, I had finally run out of them. I had made up as many exercises and dietary charts as it was possible to invent. I had weighed myself daily, and had kept running totals in my head so that I always knew, at any hour of the day, exactly how many calories I had eaten.

It had all been done in the hope of effecting some cure, yet nothing had worked, not even the knowledge and skill of professionals.

And now I was being referred to another doctor. The appointment was five days away. What if I couldn't hang on?

Without realizing it, I had gradually descended into a dangerous level of thinking, one that involved a number of self-defeating mind-sets.

For one thing, I felt totally hopeless. I had become so accustomed to my inner pain and suffering that life seemed inconceivable without it.

I felt helpless in the sense that I did not believe that anything more could be done for me.

I had allowed myself to become overwhelmed by simple tasks. Whatever it was that needed to be done was more than I could manage. Unable to do everything at once, I had gradually drifted into a pattern of doing nothing at all.

And, of course, I had paid a dreadful price for this, for I saw myself as utterly despicable and worthless. Immersed in my own despondency, I had fallen into the habit of erroneously self-labelling myself.

Finally, I had lost my tolerance for any of life's inevitable frustrations. Falsely assuming that others had a gift for easily achieving their goals, I was frequently enraged over my own shortcomings, and such obstacles as I believed fate had deliberately placed in my path.

Although I fought hard against becoming ensnared in this paralyzing web of misconceptions, I knew I was rapidly losing ground. I knew it with a frightening kind of certainty when I found myself desperately hanging on.

Thursday.

Friday.

Saturday.

Sunday.

And finally, Monday. Monday, when I would be forced to face another doctor—another stranger to my problem, to whom everything would once again need to be explained. Except that I no longer had any desire to dredge up the past. The past was as much of a mystery as it had ever been. For that matter, so was the present.

On a day-to-day basis, I had no real grasp of things, no logical explanation for anything I said or did. My fluctuating moods, my erratic eating habits, all seemed to have a life of their own. On the days when I felt bad, there was no particular thing that could be blamed. On the days that I felt good, it came as a total surprise.

The thought of continuing along in this way, of fighting against an enemy that had no face, was suddenly more that I could bear. It had taken all of my energy and strength just to make it this far. And exactly where was I?

As a college student, I had had a slight weight problem, and occasional blue moods. Now, every aspect of my life, including my weight, was hopelessly out of control.

There was no denying that my overall condition had greatly deteriorated. I felt smothered by a blanket of heaviness that seemed to be crushing me from within. All around me was a dark, nameless void.

How truly incredible it was that life could actually continue around such feelings, that my outward behavior was still acceptable enough to allow me to get by.

While I tried to think optimistically about my appointment with another doctor, most of the time, it was hard to even think. My thoughts were hopelessly fragmented, flitting here and there like jagged bolts of lightning.

Had I been able to concentrate upon any single thing, I might actually have managed to accomplish something. As it was, I could only lie in bed and fret about all the things I knew I should be doing.

What was I really capable of doing? Perhaps I should take out the garbage. Or bring in the mail.

As I toyed with the thought of doing these things, I suddenly thought about suicide. Suicide was something more than just a word. It was an option. A permanent solution to things.

Everything else was merely speculation and talk. On Monday, if I went to see my new doctor, that was what we would do—sit and talk. I would tell him my tired little tale and he would nod his head and sympathize with me. Or appear to be sympathizing. Afterwards, acting on some theory of his own, he would prescribe a method of treatment. He would urge me to be positive and hopeful, something I had lost all ability to be.

Actually, that was it—I no longer wanted to be!

61

Living was a tedious business, a constant pretense of one sort or another.

I had pretended to be a good wife.

A normal child.

A functional person.

But what was I really?

Tired.

Tired and ready to sleep.,

Counting out my prescription for Restoril, I saw that there were fifteen tablets available. Available and waiting.

On a plane trip back home, I had once taken one of these sleeping pills, and afterwards, could not remember changing planes along the way.

Yes, fifteen of them would be enough to do the job. But not until Sunday. Sunday, Larry would be on call, and I would be home alone.

As it happened, that particular Sunday was also Mother's Day. Had I stopped to consider this, it might have been enough to change my mind, but as it was, I had already begun to formulate a plan. A plan that would relieve me of any further need to constantly struggle and fail. In the process, I would also be able to unburden others. At first, they would feel badly, but that was only to be expected. Later, it would undoubtedly occur to them that what I had done was the best solution for everyone involved.

This, then, was to be my final coping mechanism—the final one, and the only one that had ever worked.

◆ ◆ ◆ ◆

6

I swallowed the Restoril tablets over a period of an entire day. After taking a couple, I crawled into bed and slept. When I awoke, I took a couple more.

Once, it was the telephone that woke me. A voice on the other end identifying itself as "your friend, Margie," asked if everything was all right. I must have sounded a little fuzzy and strange for her to ask that.

"Oh yes," I told her. "I'm fine. Everything's fine."

Not believing it, Margie stopped by to visit and we actually managed a conversation of sorts. Afterwards, she went away, and I took a few more Restoril.

The next thing I remember is lying in bed, watching Larry and Margie, who were suddenly both in the room, talking together in low, anxious tones.

When they realized I was awake, they immediately suggested that I go into a hospital. As Larry presented some logical arguments for this, Margie began to pack me a bag. Each time she left the room, I would walk over to the suitcase, and removing all the items she had packed, put them back into my closet.

In the midst of all this, my doctor called and asked if I would like for him to come over. I told him no, that everything was all right.

A while later, I received another call, this time from a therapist that Margie had been seeing. I remember that this therapist had the most wonderfully soothing voice and that it made me feel a whole lot better just listening to her. That night I slept like a log, and the following morning, I returned to work. There is little I remember about that day, except for the fact that such familiar items as pencils, paper, and coffee cups were difficult to control. Later, I would look at the notations I had made in various files and find myself wondering whose handwriting it was.

At noon, Larry arrived to take me to my first appointment with my new doctor, a psychopharmacologist.

During our initial consultation, this doctor opened a large medical book and asked me to review various symptoms I saw listed there, and to advise him of any I could specifically identify with. After that, we talked a bit more, and then Larry was called into the room.

At this stage, the doctor's function was basically that of a consultant.

Once Larry and I had returned home, it occurred to me that I had plane reservations at midnight, for I had planned to visit my sister, Beth. But in view of all that had happened, Larry urged me to check into Camelback Hospital instead. This was a local psychiatric hospital that was only a short distance away. Seeing how distraught Larry was, I immediately agreed to go.

When we arrived there, we filled out all the necessary forms, and then sat and talked until a nurse finally appeared. At that point, Larry left, and I was taken to a nearby nurse's station where my temperature and blood pressure were taken. After that, my purse was searched for any items or medications that might prove harmful to me, and then I was told to remove my clothes so that a strip search could be performed.

When I refused to allow this, my previous doctor was called and we talked briefly about the standard procedures employed by psychiatric hospitals.

"I don't care," I told him. "I'm not going to be strip searched and that's all there is to it."

The hospital, of course, would not permit me to remain unless I did exactly as they asked—so I left.

Calling a taxi, I told the driver that I only had a five dollar bill and asked him to take me as far as he could. After walking the short distance that remained, I let myself into the house and, a few minutes later, Larry arrived.

As he drove into the yard, he saw me standing at the door and stared at me in disbelief.

"Don't worry," I told him, as he came up the walk. "Everything's okay. I just couldn't stay in that place. But, I promise, I'll never do anything foolish again."

Once I explained what had happened at the hospital, Larry more or less resigned himself to the decision I had made. After all, there was very little else he could do.

A few days later, I visited the doctor who had referred me to my psychiatrist and learned that they had consulted with one another and decided that I must be manic-depressive. Although it had not worked for me before, I was urged to go back on Lithium, which this time, was to be taken in conjunction with another anti-depressant drug.

I agreed to give it a try, then returned home, where I once again made preparations to fly back to North Carolina to visit with my sister.

After arriving there, Beth arranged things so that she and I would have some quiet times together. One day, as we walked together in the woods, I told her how badly things had been going for me, and how I had found it impossible to go on. It was not until I began to explain it all that it suddenly occurred to me that I had actually attempted to take my own life!

Looking at Beth, I saw that she was as she had always been—the way I had once been myself. Raised in the same house, we had many shared experiences to reflect upon. We were so much alike, so totally in agreement on most things—except, of course, for one *particular* thing—Beth had never tried to kill herself. Somewhere along the way, we had become divided, separated forever perhaps, into categories of *normal* and *abnormal*. Whatever it actually meant to be classed as either one, it was obviously important to be seen as the former, and to avoid, at all costs, any possible association with the latter. Except that the association had already been made—by close friends and family members, who knew of my bizarre behavior, and who were becoming increasingly concerned. Their image of me was one I found I could not bear for them to have! Returning home, I once again vowed to become well.

I continued to take Lithium until the side effects became totally unbearable. When I finally com-

plained of excessive bloating and water retention, my
new doctor was totally sympathetic. Knowing that my
weight was a source of constant concern, he suggested that we delve a little deeper into the manic-
depression theory, and asked me to submit to a test.

"It's relatively new," he said, "and will require
you to go into the hospital as an out-patient."

"And what if that isn't even my problem?" I
asked.

"It will tell us that as well."

In order to obtain an accurate reading, it was
necessary for me to stop taking my Lithium and anti-
depressants for a period of two weeks before taking
the test. By the end of that time, I had managed to
lose nine pounds because of body fluids that were no
longer being retained.

Once the test had actually been administered, it
confirmed that I was not manic-depressive. On the
other hand, it revealed a dysfunctional thyroid. Sub-
clinical hypothryoidism was what it was called, and
what it referred to was a deficient activity of the
thyroid gland, a disorder that was often characterized
by a retarded rate of metabolism, resulting in somewhat sluggish behavior, and the ability to gain
weight easily on relatively small amounts of food.

I was elated at this news, nothwithstanding the
fact that my doctor seemed to feel that we had un-
covered only part of the problem.

A new medication I was given soon activated my
metabolism so that I was able to maintain my weight
at 1,800 calories per day instead of 1,200. I had
mixed feelings about this since consuming anything
over 1,200 calories had always represented binging to
me. Whenever I ate the extra 600 calories, which I

was actively encouraged to do in order to avoid a sudden, severe weight loss, I would feel "Bad, bad, bad!" although what I was doing was essential to maintaining good health.

While I could not really see the good in it, I was nonetheless delighted at the thought that I had finally met a doctor I truly respected and admired.

As time went on, my feelings for him intensified. The highlight of my day was to see him, or to talk with him on the phone for, with this, came the soothing reassurance that someone truly cared about everything I felt and thought. He was extremely handsome and polished, the epitome of what I had always believed a psychiatrist should be. Or *anyone* should be.

As our visits continued, I became increasingly concerned about my appearance. I made a point of never wearing the same outfit twice, and did all I could to make myself attractive.

Once my feelings for this doctor had become altogether apparent, we discussed *transference*, a phase of therapy in which the analyst is most often identified with a parent or lover. I was told that transference of a *positive* nature was when feelings attached to the therapist were those of love or admiration. In the case of *negative transference*, these feelings consisted of hostility or envy. Often, the patient's attitude was *ambivalent*, in which case he was inclined to experience both positive and negative feelings, as children often do toward their parents.

Of course, this was not what I wanted to hear. Nor did I believe it at first. On various occasions, I sent affectionate little notes and cards to this doctor, and one day, even attempted to present him with an expensive gift, which he politely declined. I insisted it was out of gratitude for all he had done for me. He thanked me for the thought but said his acceptance of any such gift would violate professional ethics.

He was, in all respects, as totally professional in his dealings with me as it was possible to be. Even so, he continued to demonstrate a genuine concern for my feelings.

Over a period of time, I gradually began to see the situation for what it actually was. At that point I felt embarrassed and foolish. Although I did not see how our consultations could possibly continue, I was urged to accept my past behavior as part of the process of becoming well. At first, this was difficult to do, but in the end, I managed it.

My eating disorder problem, on the other hand, was not so easily resolved. One day, I suddenly found myself binging again. I was shocked to discover that this could happen since, by then, I was thoroughly convinced that I would never again fall victim to the cycle of *binging-feeling physically ill-becoming disgusted with myself-vowing never to binge again*. And yet, it happened. And once it began, the cycle continued along as before.

There were times when I was driven to telephone my doctor late at night, complaining of such overwhelming feelings of despondency that he would arrange an appointment for me on the spot.

During the next year, my medications were changed fifteen or twenty times and, each time, I would experience or possibly *imagine* some slight improvement, but never for very long.

As a counter-balance to my depression, I often flew into unexplainable rages. One such emotional outburst followed a visit from our insurance agent, who came to speak with us on the subject of life insurance. He suggested that Larry take out a million dollar policy and that a second policy, amounting to another half-million, be taken out on me.

I was appalled at the very idea. To my own way of thinking, my life had no value at all. There was no purpose I served, no specific services I rendered that Larry would need to be financially compensated for in the event of my death. Quite simply, he would be better off without me. And since he had already proved himself capable of maintaining the lifestyle we currently enjoyed, an insurance policy on me seemed like an incredible waste of money.

Incapable of presenting this argument in a calm and rational way, I ranted and raved like a maniac and afterwards, dissolved into an uncontrollable fit of trembling and tears.

At work, things were not a great deal better. Each day at CIGNA I counseled people with dietary problems similar to my own, and invariably suggested certain behavioral modifications. Although these things had never worked for me, I advised them not to keep food in the house, to eat their meals off smaller plates to create the illusion of more, to avoid candy stores and bakeries—in short, to change their way of doing certain things in an effort to discourage them from eating. Even as I talked, and they listened, I was filled with an inner contempt at the thought that I was living a lie. Of course, there were certain people who responded quite favorably to behavioral modification since, in every instance, their problem was not identical to my own. Still, I could not seem to take credit for anything that turned out well. Failure was the only word I could truly identify with.

As my period of depression began to take precedence over my binging, I sensed that I really had two problems instead of one. My moods were not necessarily affected by better eating habits, as I had originally assumed they would be. Whether I ate too much or starved myself, the mood swings continued, and on the downside, were becoming increasingly severe.

There were times when I decided I must be a hopeless case. My doctor, on the other hand, refused to believe it. As an expert chemical analyst, he felt confident that the right medication or combination of medications would eventually be found.

One day I came to his office dressed totally in black. It was a cold rainy day, and my mood was as bleak as the weather.

Our session began with the usual questions. How was my appetite? Was I sleeping well? And exercising? How was my relationship with Larry?

Once I had given my answers, my doctor asked if I could pinpoint any specific reason for my depression.

I told him I could not.

He then asked if I could tell him what would make me happy.

I said I didn't know.

The only thing I *did* know was that I had gotten myself caught in some sort of downward spiral and that there were times when I could feel it pulling at me with the force of a deadly whirlpool.

Convinced that I was suffering from a chemical imbalance, I found it difficult to believe that some answer had not yet been found. But since it hadn't been, I was beginning to suspect that it would never be.

The future, as I saw it, was some dark, nameless thing that stretched on forever, and my only desire was to get past it, to be free—to finally know what it was to want nothing, to desire and suffer nothing, to be without apprehension, loss or need.

I was closer to it than I realized.

It was October of 1986. My condition had deteriorated to a point where I was visiting my doctor more frequently—as often as three times in a single week.

Each time, he would ask me how I felt. How was my appetite? Was I exercising? Was I sleeping well? How was my relationship with Larry?

Whenever I left his office, he would pat me on the shoulder and tell me to be good.

One day in October, I could no longer *think* of a way to be good.

Or how to be anything at all.

And so, I counted out twenty-one Librium tablets instead.

Knowing what it meant—what I was once again considering—I made one final call for help.

And that was how I came to be on a plane to Boston—on my way to McLean's Psychiatric Hospital.

And so began another long and difficult journey.

7

At unguarded moments, I found myself wondering what life in an institution would be like. It was not a question I consciously invited into my thoughts for I was more inclined to think about the time beyond. Already, I was looking forward to the day of my release, jumping ahead to that moment—whenever it might be—when my problems would finally be resolved.

But suddenly I found myself faced with another problem—the problem of being admitted. I arrived in Boston only to learn that there were no immediate beds available at McLean's.

Not knowing what I should do next, I consulted my brother. His suggestion was that I stay with him for the weekend and that on Monday morning, we renew our efforts to get me admitted to McLean's. Not wanting to leave me alone on my first night in Boston, Ken suggested I accompany him to a formal black tie dinner. He explained that it was a fund-raising affair he had planned to attend and felt that I should come along.

The idea appealed to me as an ironic, even comical twist of fate. I imagined myself dressing in something fashionably elegant and moving among a crowd of beautiful people as if I actually belonged there. And who would know that I didn't? The thought of playing this deceptive role was simply too much to resist. So on my first evening in Boston, that was exactly what I did. I had mixed feelings about it for, of course, I had been prepared to enter McLean's that day, and now I would have to prepare myself again.

On Sunday, my parents arrived from Fall River. We spent the day exploring the city which, in autumn, was a truly spectacular sight. And the Red Sox, as American League champions, had managed to add some color and excitement of their own. Wherever we looked, we saw street vendors peddling Red Sox memorabilia. On impulse, I purchased a T-shirt to send to my husband, Larry. I hoped it might somehow make him feel a little less abandoned.

I found myself suddenly overwhelmed with thoughts of Larry, and all that I wanted to do and be for him. I could not help but wonder why he had stayed with me so long. It seemed to me that he had derived little pleasure from our relationship. Luckily, in spite of my problems, his career had prospered, affording him something positive to think about each day. Perhaps that was why he was still with me—and fortunately, not *against* me.

I thought of the suicide note I had left for him a year earlier, in which I apologized for being less than he deserved. Having seen it and read it, he would always carry it with him now. No matter what else happened between us, there was no way to erase its ominous message.

And what of my mother, who would have her own special reasons for remembering the day on which I decided to take my life—May 11, 1985—

74

Mother's Day! How many years of flowers, cards and family get-togethers would there need to be before that day would hold some pleasant associations for her again?

I found I could not bear the thought of hurting people anymore than I had. McLean's would have to be the answer.

Throughout the following week, I called the admissions office on a daily basis. Each time, I was told: "No beds yet. Call back tomorrow."

I began to wonder if this was really a blessing in disguise since, in some ways I did not even feel up to being admitted to McLean's. Because I had discontinued all of my medications, except for my thyroid pills, certain symptoms of withdrawal had begun to take effect. I found myself feeling somewhat muddled and unfocused, particularly during the morning hours. One day, as I walked toward a quaint little corner market in Boston's Back-Bay area, I found myself moving in slow motion. Realizing I had lost the ability to gauge distances, or the speed of a moving car, I forced myself to cross Commonwealth Avenue in unison with other pedestrians, relying upon their judgment now rather than my own to get us safely across. There were times when everything required a great deal of effort, often exacting a higher price than I was willing to pay.

At night, I was plagued with horrible nightmares, another apparent symptom of withdrawal. Dreading the thought of being besieged by those monstrous images that paraded before me each night, I would find myself fighting sleep for as long as I could. But then, after three days, the nightmares suddenly stopped. And on the heels of that, McLean's finally advised that they would have accommodations available on Friday of that same week.

On Friday morning, I went shopping for a variety of personal items that I knew I would be needing. As always, the shopping mall was crowded, filled with people of all ages who poured in and out of the stores in a steady stream. It occurred to me that there were surely others in this place who were suffering from severe depression, people who did not yet know the true nature of their problem, but who had begun to sense, however vaguely, that something was very, very wrong. Yes, it *was* possible to suddenly know that—even while shopping for underwear, or toothpaste. And *knowing* it meant moving toward a day that would inevitably lead to some irreversible decision—something one could dread but no longer change.

For me, that moment was at hand. How totally ridiculous it would have seemed if I had suddenly insisted that I did not want to be admitted to McLean's. And yet I didn't, and knew that I didn't, even as the car advanced slowly toward the entrance to this institution.

It wasn't only one building, as I had imagined it would be, but actually, a number of buildings, both old and new, scattered over a broad expanse of lawn. There were flowers and shrubs, and many old and stately trees. It was not an unattractive place but I was nonetheless apprehensive about entering it.

Before going in, I sat in the car and cried, wondering what I had done in bringing myself here. What if this didn't work, as so many other things had not?

Still fretting over a number of painful questions, I finally entered the place and told them who I was. A short while later I was redirected to another facility, where I was told I would need to wait in the foyer until a doctor and nurse became available to admit me.

It was at this point that my parents and I said our tearful goodbyes. Afterwards, my brother Ken and I sat together quietly, observing all the people who were milling about. Most of them were smoking or drinking coffee, and there was really no way of telling the employees from the visitors or the "inmates." As these people looked back at us, I couldn't help but wonder if they were wondering too. Quite possibly, they were already making bets on which one of us would be leaving and who would be left behind.

Oh God, I thought, I don't belong here! I couldn't *possibly*! But if not here, then where? Nothing I had tried on the outside had proven to be of any help. I was here because I hadn't yet found the answer. Perhaps someone in this place, someone who was walking by at this very moment, would know exactly what to do.

"Why, of course!" I could imagine this astute individual saying. "It's not nearly as bad as you think. An unfortunate situation, to be sure, but relatively easy to treat. We'll have you out of here in no time."

As I attempted to cheer myself with these thoughts, I was suddenly relieved of my luggage and other items I had brought with me, and these were secured at the nurse's station. After that, I was taken into an interview room to meet with a psychiatric resident. Although I hadn't thought it would be possible, Ken was allowed to accompany me.

77

At that point, I was asked to give a detailed account of the past fifteen years—all that had happened, all that I felt had contributed to that one desperate moment in which I had once again come to the brink of suicide.

It occurred to me as I sat there explaining it, that I sounded entirely too upbeat. For the moment, that was the way I felt, but I knew it was also part of a cycle that ebbed and flowed like the tide, causing me to feel highly exhilarated at times, generally, just before it plunged me down into the darkest depths of despair. I wondered if this doctor would sense that the way I sounded had little to do with the way I actually was. Although I could sit and chat casually with him, as if the things we were discussing were of no real consequence, I was nonetheless a product and a victim of these things. Still, the inclination was constantly there to laugh off my more bizarre behavior—*I used to keep these charts, Doctor—I wish you could see them—stacks and stacks of charts itemizing every bite of food I ate, every form of exercise I indulged in. I don't have any idea what I intended to prove with all that, but anyway, I still have those charts. Maybe I should paper my walls with them!*

I would subsequently learn that one of the more harmful aspects of my tendency toward self-deprecation was that it belittled some of my most valiant efforts to remain a truly functional individual. Such coping mechanisms as I had invented through the years were really all I had during my darkest periods of despair. Later, psychiatrists would tell me that they did not believe I would have survived without that willful determination to keep myself on the track. Granted, nothing I tried had really worked.

But for the time I was preoccupied with trying to make it work, I was acting out some positive role. I was determined to take control, to change, to improve, to heal myself. In each case, I hadn't done the right thing—but at least it was *something*.

Once my initial interview at McLean's had ended, it was time for Ken to leave. We did not prolong the moment since this would only have made it harder.

"Don't worry," he said, "you'll be out of here soon."

"Sooner than you think," I insisted, in an effort to convince us both.

After my brother had gone, and while I was still attempting to reconcile myself to the fact that I was actually in this place, a nurse and the psychiatric resident showed me to my room.

At this point, every item in my luggage and purse were carefully inspected, and I was immediately deprived of such things as my razor, my hair dryer and tape recorder, since these were all electrical things that had to be approved by the hospital's mechanical staff. Other small items that were also taken included a pocket scissors and a nail file.

Once this had been done, I was left to myself for a while and took this opportunity to look around the room. Such meager furnishings as there were to be found included an unmade bed, one chair, one dresser, one desk, and a window that had been permanently secured with a heavy screen.

I was alone. A few minutes passed—and then a few more. I could feel a wave of anxiety starting to build inside me, something I knew I would need to control if I hoped to get out of here. Since I had been deprived of every conceivable object with which I could possibly harm myself, I was obviously not to be trusted. *Did these people think I was crazy?!* If they did, then undoubtedly they had only been humoring me with their questions. I went back over my answers, trying to imagine how they must have sounded to someone who was looking for signs of neuroticism or psychosis. I thought I had behaved rather well. But wasn't that altogether typical of someone who was actually quite balmy? Perhaps I had impressed them as a person who was exerting a tremendous amount of effort to appear normal. And why not? I had often been guilty of role-playing, of acting happier, calmer, and certainly more in control than I was. Fooling these people would not be as easy as fooling one's loved ones and friends. Someone who was close to you had a natural tendency to filter out all the negative information, permitting themselves to see only what was right and good in you. But here were doctors and nurses who were finely attuned to all that was abnormal in a patient—however subtle the outward signs might be.

All right now, calm down! I thought. *You're here to get better. And you will. How serious can your problem be if you've managed to function for all these years? So many others who are here cannot function in the outside world at all. Even at your worst, you're still better off than THEY are.*

That first night, I lay in bed and stared up at the ceiling. The moon was out. Its cold, bluish-white light streamed in through the mesh on my window. Every five minutes, a staff member came into the room and checked on me. Although many had complained about this constant invasion of privacy, I found it oddly reassuring. The following week, when I was advised that my check time had been moved back to every fifteen minutes, I very nearly saw it as a sign of neglect.

As I gradually became less self-absorbed and more interested in my immediate surroundings, I learned that there were twenty-five patients assigned to our floor. Most were there because of some affective disorder. Some, like myself, had been assigned to private rooms while others co-existed with another patient. The worst cases, the ones most inclined to harm themselves, were confined to "quiet rooms." These rooms, which were generally quite dark, encouraged the patient to sleep a great deal of the time on a mattress in the middle of the floor.

As I became a little better acquainted with my new "instant family," I discovered that mental illness was no respecter of age or position. Here there were people of every age, both educated and uneducated. Some were wealthy. Some were not. Many held college degrees, and there were a number of professional executives. I could not help but wonder what had brought all these people here, and whether or not they had actually improved.

It was somewhat unnerving to finally be exposed to those with more serious mental disorders. In one case, a patient's fit of hysteria was triggered by a fire drill. Later I would learn that her own daughter had perished in a fire and that this had been the cause for her wild and uncontrollable behavior. By the time she was finally sedated, I was ready to be tranquilized as well. The shock of actually seeing a person unable to maintain any control over their mind or emotions was both frightening and thoroughly incom-

81

prehensible to me. Throughout most of my life. I had fought to maintain control, had battled my own weakness and compulsions in both logical and illogical ways. Whatever I had done had been done with the thought that I *must* come to grips with myself, that I must somehow overpower whatever was overpowering me. The object was to hang on, to try whatever there was to be tried, but to never give up or give in. As a product of this rigid sort of thinking, I found it appalling that a woman could become totally unravelled, merely at the sound of a bell.

These people were sick, really sick! A number of them had been here for several years. What was I doing among them? For a moment, I could not catch my breath. I felt my heart leap into my throat.

Returning to my room, I sat at the window and stared outside. Outside had suddenly become an inaccessible place, for now I was in a locked ward, where every move was closely monitored. It was a fairly isolated form of existence. All I had was a book to read and a Walkman on which to listen to music. Since my meals were also delivered to the floor, my only real exposure to people was during those times when I would sit in the foyer.

Listening to others talk, I would invariably conclude that their problems were much "bigger and better" than mine. Or to put it another way, they seemed to be involved in some far greater confusion, for I simply did not know how to control my erratic eating habits, and as far as I knew, that was the only problem I had.

One day, I sat down next to a small group of women, hoping to become better acquainted, as the hospital staff regularly encouraged us to do. I was

82

deeply hurt when these women immediately moved to another part of the room. I saw only one way to interpret their actions and that was in terms of rejection. Later, I would learn that they had been engaged in a private discussion. Their actions hadn't really been directed against me. Why was I always inclined to think the worst of myself? It was true. I was guilty of that.

Unfortunately, I was not yet aware that I frequently engaged in *emotional reasoning*, allowing myself to assume that my emotional reactions were, in fact, an accurate reflection of the way things were. If I felt that people were snubbing me, then that was what they were doing. It hadn't yet occurred to me to consider an alternative. In my own mind, it was as if no other alternatives even existed.

I have no doubt that such feelings were at least partially responsible for my early tendency to maintain some distance between myself and the other patients on the floor. But my brother soon brought an end to this, for he was extremely outgoing, and demonstrated great interest in everyone and the circumstances that had brought them there. Ken conversed with all the patients in a warm and friendly manner, which quickly encouraged them to open up and share their life experiences.

"Let's go out into the foyer," he would invariably say as soon as he arrived. And while I frequently insisted that I did not care for all the noise and smoke, I would always end up following along.

One day Ken asked a staff member if he could take me out on the grounds for a walk. He was told that this would not be allowed until my doctor had personally approved it.

83

"I don't get it," Ken said to me later. "Where in the world do they think you're going to run off to?"

I explained to him that in a place like McLean's, trust was not simply bestowed upon you. It had to be earned.

"You gradually become entitled to certain privileges," I told him, "and these are increased as your condition continues to improve. 'A' privileges, for example, entitle you to keep your appointments and to go to the cafeteria on your own. 'B' privileges allow you to incorporate some extra-curricular activities into your daily schedule. At that point, you might attend exercise or art classes, although it's extremely important to remember to sign off the floor. They always want to know where you are."

"Well, when do they finally allow you to get a breath of fresh air around here?" Ken asked, still a trifle annoyed at the staff's refusal to allow me a little more freedom.

"That's another part of 'C' privileges," I told him. "And finally, there are 'D' privileges, which actually allow you to leave the grounds for certain specified periods. Don't worry, Ken. It won't be long before we'll be able to do all those things together."

Determined to make good on my promise, I managed to work my way up to 'D' privileges within a matter of one or two weeks. This, in itself, it seemed to me, was a fair indication that my condition had greatly improved.

In a manner of speaking, I was the perfect candidate for a rigidly structured existence since, even on the outside, I had spent so many years structuring every hour of every day. Unlike other patients, who were frequently uncooperative, I was quick to adapt and happy to abide by the rules since I was only content if my day was carefully planned, and if each task was executed on a timely basis, and to everyone's satisfaction—including my own.

Although patients were not allowed out of bed before 6:00 a.m., they were also not allowed to remain in bed after 8:00 a.m. It was possible to take an afternoon nap between the hours of 2:00 p.m. and 4:00 p.m., but simply lying around in bed was not condoned, unless, of course, a patient was physically ill.

During the night, regular bed checks continued, with a constant parade of staff members coming into the room, or pausing in doorways just long enough to shine a light in your face. I would find myself chuckling whenever I thought of how my brother Ken would've reacted to something like this.

One day I was told that my case had been permanently assigned to a psychiatric resident, whose responsibility it would be to see that I accomplished all that was necessary during my stay.

Soon after this, I was called into a meeting room where I found myself surrounded by a large group of people. They consisted of doctors, social workers, recreational therapists, medical students, nurses, and mental health workers. Seated in a large semi-circle, they observed me closely, as I once again reiterated the various events in my life that had led to my coming to McLean's. In the course of doing this, I felt obliged to emphasize one of the main reasons I had chosen to come.

"It was my hope that I would be able to undergo a beam scan," I told them, "since I know it's now possible to monitor a person's brain waves and deter-

85

mine if there is some physiological reason for extreme fluctuations in mood and behavior. Incidentally, I think I should point out that I'm a little pressed for time. You see, I really need to get back to Phoenix as I have a job waiting for me there."

Although there was no outward reaction to my words, I have no doubt that these people were highly amused to think that I would actually impose a time limit upon their efforts to make me well. But, of course, I was imposing the same time limit upon myself. As I saw it, if they were willing to cure me by a certain date, then I was perfectly willing to be healed within that same time frame. It all seemed very fair and logical to me.

I had hoped to be released from McLean's within three weeks, but as the third week drew to a close, I realized I would need to change the date of my return flight home. It was to be the first of many such changes. Each time I called the airlines, I expected a reservations clerk to pick up the phone and say, "Yes, Dorie, what is it now?"

In between phone calls, I vowed to work harder at becoming well. After all, Thanksgiving would soon be here and I had made a lot of plans. Since these plans involved a number of other people, I knew they would be difficult if not impossible to change.

The doctor assigned to my case subsequently introduced me to a therapist and, after that, I was given a battery of tests. In addition to a thorough physical, which included a test for TB, my hearing was checked, and I was asked to undergo some neurological testing. Another part of my work-up included the inevitable I.Q. and ink blot tests. Afterwards, a mental health worker was assigned to me.

This was a person I could go to whenever I felt the need to talk. He also coordinated my daily activities, and provided a great deal of encouragement and support.

Through our conversations, I gradually learned the importance of *communication*—a word I had never really understood. True communication, it seemed, had nothing to do with simply mouthing words, or telling others what I felt they wanted to hear. Communicating meant telling people exactly how I felt, regardless of the consequences. We spoke about *unconditional love*, the kind a parent feels for a child, the kind that cannot be undone by mere actions or words. I was reminded that there were certainly people like that in my life—my own parents, and my husband, for example—people who cared enough to separate me from my curious and often incomprehensible behavior. After all, I *was* not the things I said and did, but rather a *person* who said and did those things. As my therapy sessions became more intensive they also became longer. One day, I actually went through six hours of therapy, which left me both mentally and emotionally drained. And yet, the sessions continued. In addition to meetings with social workers, there were family group meetings, women's group, and transition group. As taxing as it was, the constant activity and unrelenting regimentation helped me to avoid another onset of depression. Other patients who were deeply immersed in their problems, who constantly talked about them, or else, simply sat and stared into space, were amazed at my energy and drive. Each day, as we lined up in front of the medication window, some-

87

one would invariably say. "Give me whatever Dorie's taking," as if I had found some answer they had not.

My parents were equally convinced that I was totally miscast among this group, and they frequently expressed their own bewilderment with the situation as a whole.

"Just look at her!" my mother remarked to a social worker one day. "Dorie is such a beautiful girl. I can't imagine what could possibly be wrong."

Some time would pass before my parents were finally able to see beneath the surface, before they could actually penetrate the facade of that person I had always claimed to be.

When the psychiatrist assigned to my case at last expressed her own opinions, I was disheartened to hear her say that she believed my problems to be psychologically-based rather than chemically-based. This contention made me feel as if I were suddenly back to square one. For a number of years, I had felt exactly as she did. But gradually, I had come to the conclusion that some chemical imbalance in my body was the real culprit. I had *wanted* this to be true, since then, a simple change in diet, or perhaps some megadose of vitamins or medication might have been enough to set everything right again. But psychological problems—well, that was something else!

My parents could not really understand any of it, even after it had been explained to them. They simply could not conceive of anything in my childhood that might have had any adverse affects upon me. After all, I had been cared for. And loved. I had seemed happy. My life had been easy. I had done well in school. I was popular. Pretty. Where was the

88

problem in any of that? The fact was, I had much to be thankful for.

There were times when I felt compelled to assure everyone that I *was* grateful. I considered myself extremely privileged, and certainly, there was nothing I had blamed my parents for. It was just that something was wrong, and in an effort to make it right, I had sought out many forms of help.

While at McLean's, I consulted with another psychopharmacologist, a behavioralist, a therapist, whom I saw three times a week, and there was even a medical student involved in my case.

As time went on, I found I could relate the entire story of my life with almost total detachment. Having told it so many times, I was no longer emotionally involved. It was as if it had all happened to someone else.

One day I learned that a field trip had been scheduled to Walden Pond. I was extremely excited about this. When the moment of our departure arrived, I found myself making a quick walk-around inspection of the van in which we would be riding. I did not want to be seen in any vehicle that might have the name of the hospital imprinted on its sides. It was interesting to note that while I had come here for help, some part of me still refused to accept that I was a patient in a mental hospital. It made me wonder about things—about my ability to be honest with myself, and if, in fact, I was really improving.

Several times a week I would place a call to my husband, often after my brother had talked to him and told me how much Larry missed me.

Inwardly pleased and reassured by these words, I would call, but Larry never sounded the way I expected him to. More often than not, he sounded preoccupied, as if I had interrupted him at something. One evening, he even admitted that I had called in the middle of his favorite TV show.

At that, I hung up the phone and didn't call back for several days. I was stung by his callous indifference, by the fact that he could actually display a greater interest in television than he did in his wife who was confined to a mental institution.

When at last I felt calmer, I called him again, and this time, he scolded me for being so extravagant.

"You certainly loaded up our charge cards before leaving here," he said.

At that, I grew angry and spiteful. "That's exactly why I'm here!" I reminded him, no longer certain that he even understood or cared about my problems. "The over-eating, the sudden shifts in my mood—did it ever occur to you that I might be doing these things to compensate for the attention I haven't been getting from you? I've been trying so hard to talk to you, Larry, but no matter when I call, it never seems to be the right time."

Although he seemed somewhat taken aback by all this, Larry listened to what I had to say, and that evening, we talked for a very long time. We finally agreed that our marriage was in trouble, but that it was certainly worth saving, and that better communication was the key.

The next day, I received a bouquet of flowers from Larry, and after that, he became extremely attentive to my needs. I was shocked to think how easy it had been to gain his attention once a genuine effort was made. All it had taken was a frank admission of how I felt. Why had I never confessed my feelings before?

As the weeks passed, I realized there was no longer any hope of following through on plans I had made for Thanksgiving. This meant informing a close personal friend of my immediate situation, since she had planned to visit me in Arizona. It also meant that my brother and some of his friends would need to make other plans—and all because of me. At that time, I was still inclined to take the blame for whatever happened to go wrong—even as another part of me freely acknowledged that I was exactly where I needed to be, and that my health and well-being must now take precedence over everything else.

During one of my therapy sessions, the medical student assigned to my case asked a rather thought-provoking question:

"What is it exactly that makes you angry?" he wanted to know.

I thought and thought about it. "Why nothing at all," I finally said. "Unless you're referring to common everyday annoyances. Is that what you mean?"

"No," he said. "I mean things that really make you angry."

After the therapy session had ended, I continued to think about it. By nightfall, I was amazed to find that I had compiled a long list of things that made me angry. How was it that I had been able to live my entire life without acknowledging my own anger? Why had I done this? And what had it served to accomplish?

While at McLean's, I was taught to perceive anger as a totally acceptable emotion—one that actually had some therapeutic value, as long as it was

anger

properly channeled. The worst thing of all, it seemed, was to suppress and internalize anger to a point where it inevitably led to an emotional tirade, to severe depression, or even to suicide.

Feeling truly enlightened, I found I was eager to try my wings and asked when I might leave. It was then that I learned that this could not be arranged until Larry had come to Boston and personally conferred with my therapist and the social worker assigned to my case. Earlier, I had been told that Larry's visit was optional. Now it was suddenly mandatory. I was extremely disturbed by this since I felt it might further delay my release. Even so, I could see that it was important for Larry to acquaint himself with the type of treatment I had undergone, and to meet the people I had been working with.

After he arrived, we engaged in our mandatory meeting, and many important issues were discussed. I was surprised to learn that both Larry and I were inclined to keep our feelings and our problems to ourselves, assuming in advance that the other would not understand.

We talked about *unconditional love*, which is able to transcend any immediate mood or circumstance, however difficult or unpleasant it might be. We were asked if we believed our own feelings for one another were more superficial than that, if we felt that everything was "at risk" the moment we displayed some unpleasant side of ourselves. Larry did not seem to think so, and neither did I. At that point, we were reminded that the object was to *communicate*—through good times and bad, since that was what would bring us truly close.

Having come this far, I was finally able to admit that I often feared that I might make Larry angry, or fail to live up to his expectations. *me too*

"If that happened," I said, "I assumed he wouldn't like me anymore."

Another unfortunate habit of mine concerned itself with validating my existence through his. On my own, I believed I had little self-worth. But after all, I had married a doctor—or rather, a doctor had married *me*. Didn't this prove something? What I had been hoping it might prove was that I was actually pretty enough and intelligent enough to attract such an exceptional man. Although I had always been inclined to gauge my own worth on these terms, this gradually changed while I was staying at McLean's. It was while I was there that I attended my fifteen year high school reunion. I went alone, which meant that, for once, I had no one's arm to hang onto, and no one to introduce as "my husband, the doctor." Incredibly, I not only survived the experience, but actually managed to have a good time.

Since it was felt that I had made substantial progress in being able to instigate and recognize these changes in myself, it was finally decided that I should be released.

As part of a discharge summary conference, everyone involved in my care participated in a group discussion and made their individual recommendations. It was suggested that Larry and I should attend some form of Couples Counseling to reinforce our relationship, and that I should seek out a woman psychologist or psychiatrist with whom to continue my therapy. I was strongly urged to *verbalize* my feelings and to let others know exactly what it was that I needed from them. I was reminded again of the dangers of suppressing my anger and what this might ultimately lead to.

Everyone's words of advice were still churning around in my head on the day I was finally released.

My parents came to pick me up, and afterwards, we stopped for lunch. As my father walked to a nearby counter to place our pizza orders, my mother and I sat quietly in a booth. The expression on her face, when at last I took the time to notice, was one of gratitude and relief. Her child had come back to her, happy and whole again, and the ugly times were past. It was more or less what I had expected her feelings to be. But what of my own?

Suddenly I was horrified to realize that what I felt was something altogether different. Slowly, insidiously, a certain suspicion had begun to creep into my mind—the idea that perhaps I had been wounded beyond all hope of healing. The fact was, my spirits were desperately low. There was no hint of joy in my heart. There was nothing at all. Deep down inside myself I knew that not enough had changed. The problems were still there—still unresolved, still taunting me as before.

I noticed that my mother's face had grown suddenly tense and anxious, the way I had hoped it might never look again.

I felt the tears on my cheeks.

It was starting all over again!

❖ ❖ ❖ ❖

94

8

"I think I NEED to be sick!"

Here was a thought I had avoided, had not dared entertain for more than a moment whenever I allowed myself to think of it at all. I could not begin to imagine what had suddenly made me blurt it out to my psychopharmacologist, but one day I actually did.

I said it in anger. In desperation. In total despair. I had no desire to engage in an argument about it. After all, who could deny the facts? Everything possible had been done for me. I was beyond hope, beyond *everything*—including anyone's need for further concern. From this point on, I would simply drift along until drifting became impossible. Until hanging on became too much of an effort. However, it finally ended no longer seemed important. It would simply end, or I would end it, or the *world* would end. Something would happen.

As I sat there thinking these dismal thoughts, I suddenly heard the mention of someone's name.

"Karen Pitico," the psychopharmacologist was saying as he handed me a slip of paper. "Here's her address and phone number. I'd like you to make an appointment."

I stared down at the paper, trying to think of something appropriate to say. "Who is she?" I finally asked.

"She's a Cognitive Therapist. I think you should go and see her."

"Why? I don't even know what cognitive therapy is."

"I'd rather have her explain that."

I thought of all the different forms of therapy I had already undergone and how none of them had really helped. I still wasn't cured. I was the same Dorie, the same dysfunctional binge eater I had been for more than half my life. Even so, I found I was still willing to try, if there was anything left to be tried.

I went home and called Karen Pitico. After that, I quickly consulted my dictionary. Reading what Webster had to say didn't tell me much. *Cognition*, according to the dictionary, was the process of knowing in the broadest sense. *Knowing in the broadest sense.* Knowing what? Myself? But that was the whole problem. I already knew myself. And I didn't like anything I knew.

Karen Pitico, as I eventually learned, had a Master's Degree in Counseling and Personnel, as well as a Master's in Social Work. She had begun working in Phoenix, Arizona in 1976 at the Maricopa Medical Center. In 1985, she became the Coordinator of the Special Psychotherapy Clinic in their Department of Psychiatry, where she organized various groups concerned with anxiety, panic, stress, and also, a number of women's problems.

I decided to see a Cognitive Therapist as a last-ditch effort, hoping that maybe there still existed some kind of therapy that would finally work. Maybe this would be it. I didn't know.

Early on in our discussions, Karen drew up a little chart for me. In final form, it looked like this:

A	B	C
Situations	Beliefs	Consequences
Events	Thoughts	Behaviors
	Assumptions	Feelings
	Expectations	
	Values	
	Philosophy of Life	

As Karen explained it, it was not so much what *happened* to me (Column A), but how I viewed the situation (Column B) which, in turn, determined the consequences (Column C).

These concepts were new to me, and as the truth slowly registered, something clicked. Eating was a compulsion based on my lack of control, my low self-esteem and lack of self-worth. *more positively*

The object of the chart was to help me RE-structure my perceptions of daily events so that I could see them realistically. Then, and only then, would I be able to act or react in a manner that was both rational and appropriate to the circumstances involved.

Another thing Karen explained was that I had options and alternatives. That there was more than one way to look at a problem, and certainly more than one way of dealing with it.

As Karen talked, I thought back to my periods of binging. Once I had opened a box of cookies, it had never occurred to me to eat only one or two. For me,

97

it had always been the entire box. Why? *Because I felt I had no choice!* I couldn't stop with just one candy bar. I ate until it made me sick.

Sweets weren't the only foods I indulged in. Cashews, bagels, potato chips, rolls, cheese, crackers—whatever was handy. I would buy a dozen bagels at a time. By the time I got home, I had already eaten three. As I carefully cut and wrapped the rest to put in the freezer, another two disappeared. I could actually eat a dozen bagels at a time. I didn't know how to stop.

When I wanted something to eat—I wanted it now. I couldn't be bothered with taking the time to prepare food. When Larry and I bought our home in Arizona, I wasn't nearly as worried about the size of the mortgage payment as I was about the microwave, for now, I could heat up just about anything in record time. The microwave could make things even worse than they already were.

I learned how to fill my stomach efficiently. Liquids took up too much space, and so I avoided them, as well as fruits and vegetables, except as a last resort.

My shopping style was quite different from that of other grocery store customers. I walked up and down the aisles searching for something . . .I didn't know what I wanted that could satisfy me. I would pick up a bag of chips and then put it back on the shelf. I would do the same in the cookie aisle, making selections and then changing my mind. Some days, after 30 minutes of shopping, I would walk out of the store empty-handed. I felt compelled to buy food to satisfy my urge to binge, but something inside me knew that there really was nothing here that could satisfy the hunger within me. It wasn't really food I was craving.

I knew every convenience store in the city, not only its location, but also its personnel, and delivery schedules. One store might have particularly fresh candy bars, another stocked the best chips, a third carried homemade cookies. If cookies were delivered fresh on Thursday afternoon, I was sure to be there. I planned my day around convenience store delivery schedules. I had to be at the one on 56th Street at 9:00 a.m. to pick up chips. I never accepted appointments until 9:30 on that morning.

My own thoughts, assumptions, and expectations about myself (Column B) were such that I was obliged to play out the role of a "binger." Believing I WAS that kind of person made it necessary to conjure up the appropriate feelings and behavior patterns. Binging (Column C-Consequences) was the inevitable result.

Karen said to me, "Dorie, you don't have to binge." As simple as it was, I had never really understood that I had this choice. During the years that the Hunger and Self-Loathing drove me to eat, I was not in control. Hunger was in control. I had been waging a losing battle with this inner monster without stopping to think what it was that the monster actually represented. Up, down, back, forth, push, pull, to and fro—the monster either advanced and controlled me or retreated and left me momentarily alone. When Karen told me "You don't have to binge," it shocked me into realizing that I really could change things. *I could be in control!*

99

As I sat and stared at the little chart that Karen had drawn, I began to understand the relationship between Columns A and B, and also B and C.

Situation: The availability of a box of cookies
Belief: I am a chronic overeater
Consequence: I eat the box of cookies.

In order to change the end result, it would first be necessary to alter my beliefs.

Situation: The availability of a box of cookies
Belief: I am in control. My first decision is to
                 eat healthy foods, but if I want a
                 cookie, I can have one and be satisfied.
Consequence: I eat one or two cookies.

Inwardly, I was extremely excited but I was also somewhat wary. Could it really be that simple? Could *anything* be? After all I had gone through, everything that had brought me to this point, all the treatments and various forms of therapy that hadn't worked—it hardly seemed possible. Even so, I felt highly elated to think that I actually had *choices*! Choices, options, and alternatives. Things COULD change. They did not need to stay the same.

If this would appear to be an overly-simplistic approach to a problem of sixteen years standing, let me pose the following question:

As regards *anything* in your life that is presently making you unhappy—your job, your personal relationships, etc., do you feel that you would like to make some changes, if only you could? If circumstances allowed it? If the opportunity were only there? If

100

that is how you perceive your problem, or possibly even your life, you are saying, in effect, that *you have no choice.*

Many people feel that way. And while they may be outwardly resigned to whatever it is they feel they cannot change, inside themselves, changes may already be taking place. Changes in the state of their health, in their attitudes, in their outlook on life. Changes that frequently cause them to feel angry or depressed.

As a product of many such self-destructive changes, I was literally overwhelmed to discover that I actually had choices. Choices I had never acted upon. I could CHANGE things. In fact—I was the only one who *could*!

"You've been extremely critical of your own behavior." Karen observed one day. "Do you see anything wrong in that?"

I thought for a moment, then slowly shook my head. "No. My habits are obviously the source of all my problems. I do terrible things. Things I know are wrong. Things I hate myself for afterwards. And yet, I keep doing them."

"But your behavior isn't even the issue, Dorie. What you really need to be focusing on is your thoughts."

"My thoughts?"

"That's right. What do you feel is *responsible* for your behavior? You act according to the way you *think*, the way you view and interpret your life situations. Had it ever occurred to you that you might be giving yourself false information?"

101

"Yes, I've thought of that," I said, and once again reflected upon my feelings about food—about having to eat an entire box of cookies, because that was the sort of person I was. But what if it wasn't really true? What if I'd only been selling myself a bill of goods? "My whole life is falling apart."

"How about 'I'm a chronic over-eater'?" I asked with a smile.

"Yes, how *about* that? Do you think this was the case when you were eating so little that you actually became anorexic? Of course not. It's wrong to make any sort of blanket statement about yourself. Wrong, and often quite dangerous."

"Well, there's no denying that I've done it," I said. "What other forms of erroneous thinking do people engage in?

"They tend to ignore the positive. Whatever they've managed to accomplish amounts to nothing in their minds because of one thing they somehow failed to do. Ignoring the positive causes you to dwell on your shortcomings to such a degree that you can no longer see anything good in yourself."

Bingo! Once again, the message struck home. Suddenly, I began to suspect that I would see myself in every example that Karen gave. And so I did.

After our session had ended, I returned home and thought about the various categories of faulty thinking that we had discussed.

Personalizing was another one, the tendency to relate oneself to an event when there is little or no basis for making this connection. "Everybody is looking at me." It made me think of an incident that had happened at McLean's, when the group of women I had wanted to befriend had suddenly moved away from me. Personalizing this incident, I had immediately assumed that they were rejecting me, when in fact, they had simply wanted to discuss a private matter.

Either-Or thinking was yet another means of falsely programming oneself. "Either I'll go on vacation in two weeks or I won't go anywhere at all." How often had I said to myself (particularly as a teenager), "If I can't have (that dress), (that car), (that boy), I'll simply die!" Young people are criticized for taking such an absolutist's view of things, but adults do it too. Looking back over my life, I could think of any number of things I had once considered important, even vital to my happiness. Without question, they would NOT have been the right things for me to have, or the right people for me to associate with. Therein lies the real danger of Either-Or thinking.

Another unfortunate habit is one that cause us to *Magnify or Minimize* issues or events. How often had my concerns or anxieties been totally out of proportion to what the immediate situation warranted? By the same token, I had often been inclined to minimize faults in myself or in others, glossing them over in a way that made them more acceptable to me.

And what of *Emotional Reasoning*? "This is the way I feel about it, so it must be true." Yes, I was certainly inclined to make emotional decisions. Rarely did I make any other kind.

Finally, I was guilty of haranguing myself with an endless list of *Shoulds and Shouldn'ts*, mentally whipping myself for things I either did or did not do.

103

All it had ever accomplished was to plunge me into deeper and deeper states of depression.

The good news in all this, according to Karen, was that I was doing these things to myself. That also meant that I could stop doing them. Without question, it was possible for me to gain greater insight into each situation and then control or restructure my thought patterns in order to arrive at a different result.

I began by carefully guarding and analyzing my thoughts. For any who have never done this, particularly those who consider themselves to be basically optimistic and cheerful, I must warn you that you may be surprised! If you dutifully monitor your thoughts throughout the course of a day, you will be amazed at how often you are inclined to feed yourself negative information.

Example:

Morning

1. There isn't enough coffee here to make a full cup. How could I have forgotten to buy some? I'm ALWAYS doing that! (Exaggerated Thinking)
Correct Thinking: The fact is, I'm not *always* doing that. I do it sometimes, just as anyone will.

2. This is going to be a terrible day. It's starting off all wrong! (Emotional Reasoning)

Correct Thinking: The way I feel has nothing to do with the day. The sun came up this morning just as it always does. The birds are singing. The air is clear and cool. The day itself is lovely, but something inside me is not. I'd better take a closer look at this and see what's actually responsible for my mood.

Afternoon

1. I don't know why I come to this restaurant for lunch. I always seem to get that one waitress who doesn't like me. (Personalizing)

Correct Thinking: The waitress has no reason to dislike me. It's true that she's sometimes brusque and impatient but that's the way she is with everyone. Perhaps she's unhappy or troubled about something, just as I have often been.

2. As much as I'd like to, I can't eat a pasta salad. I've got to start thinking about my weight. (Shoulds and Shouldn'ts)

Correct Thinking: If I eat this now, I can eat something lighter this evening. A plain omelet and some toast might be nice.

Evening

1. That insurance check didn't come in the mail today. If it isn't here by tomorrow, I'm sure I'll never get it. Obviously, the company doesn't want to pay on my claim. (Either-Or Thinking)

Correct Thinking: My agent assured me that the claim had been approved. Isn't it possible that the check could be lying on someone's desk, just waiting to be signed?

2. I hope I manage to get some sleep tonight. I don't know why I should suddenly be troubled with insomnia. Oh well, it isn't such a big thing, Other people have much worse problems. (Minimization)

Correct Thinking: The fact is, I've *never* been troubled with insomnia. This is obviously a sign that something is wrong in my life. Whatever it is, I can't afford to ignore it at the expense of my health and well-being. Maybe it's time to take a closer look at the way I feel about my job.

Through Cognitive Therapy, I hoped to learn how to cope in appropriate ways. My *own* coping mechanisms (and certainly there had been many), had never been particularly appropriate to my needs. What sense had there been in recording every bite of food that went into my mouth? The food was not the problem, not anymore than my mouth was. The problem existed in the *thought processes* that triggered the behavior. If those thoughts could only be changed, then perhaps a lot of other things could be changed as well.

What an exciting and challenging idea this was! I found I could hardly wait to put it to the test.

At Karen's request, I agreed to monitor my days on the basis of the A-B-C chart she had drawn. She asked that I keep track of (A) the situations and events that occurred throughout the week. The (B's)—my thoughts, beliefs, expectations and assumptions about these situations and events would also need to be recorded, as would (C), my resultant feelings and behaviors.

The purpose of all this was to clearly analyze what I was doing each day (doing to myself) so that I could draw some realistic conclusions:

Was I confusing thought with fact?

Was I exaggerating?

Was I overgeneralizing?

Was I ignoring the positive?

What were the consequences of my thoughts?

And finally, what were my options and alternatives?

Karen repeatedly warned me that people, like animals, are creatures of habit. "If you don't think so," she said, "try doing things differently if you can. Tomorrow morning, notice the normal little rituals you go through, the order in which you shower, brush your teeth, comb your hair and get dressed. Then try to change the order in which you do these things and see if you experience any feeling of inner resistance."

Without even having undertaken this experiment, I already knew that I would. When I admitted this, Karen nodded and smiled.

"So, what you're saying is—I've worked out a routine, and since I've been using it for years, I see no reason to change it."

"Yes, I'd say that's true."

"Even if another way worked better?"

"Well, I really hadn't thought about that—I mean, that there might be a better way of getting my day started."

"But isn't it possible that there is?"

"Yes, of course."

107

"And yet you'd rather stay with the routine you've already established."

"I suppose I would. Mostly because it's comfortable. And familiar."

"Exactly. Now then, Dorie, let me ask you this. If I promised to give you a million dollars for changing your morning ritual, would you be willing to do it?"

"Well, sure!"

"Money is a tremendous motivator, isn't it? Even greater than our desire to overcome negative and self-defeating habits that have been dragging us down."

"I suppose that's true."

"I only wish that it weren't. If you could be the way you've always wanted to be, the person you've been *striving* to be for all these many years—or if you could have a million dollars—which would you choose?"

"I see what you mean," I said. "Most people would immediately equate one with the other. Once I have a million dollars, everything else will magically resolve itself."

"Do you think it would?"

"No."

"And you'd be right. You would still be a product of all your experiences, and your own cognitive impressions and interpretations of those events. They would continue to mislead you into feeling and behaving as you do. By your own admission, Dorie, many of your past behaviors have left you feeling angry, depressed, frustrated and totally without hope. On more than one occasion, you've described yourself as a 'terrible person'. Believing this has only compounded your anger and frustration, making you

108

feel all the more terrible about yourself, and also, about your life in general. As a product of these negative thoughts, it's really doubtful that the acquisition of a million dollars would make that much difference. In fact, you would probably be inclined to see yourself as a terrible person who suddenly, through some fluke, managed to acquire a fortune, something they hadn't done anything to earn. A terrible person could only feel guilty and ashamed about that, believing themselves to be totally undeserving."

"I'm afraid you've described me perfectly," I said, somewhat discomfited by the fact that Karen should know me so well.

"I haven't described you at all," she responded with a smile. "Only the way you think about yourself."

"If that's true," I countered, desperately hoping that it was, "then obviously I need to start changing my thoughts."

"What Cognitive Therapy is more concerned with," Karen explained, "is the actual *development* of thought, and that is why I've asked you to fill out the A-B-C chart. I want you to become critically aware of your thought processes—how you *assimilate* thought as a result of the situations and events that occur. Then I'd like you to think about how your reactions are affecting you. If you do a really thorough job of this, at first, you may have time for little else. But I'd urge you to give this exercise a high priority in your life since, in a very real sense, it *is* your life, or what your life will ultimately become."

There it was—the long and the short of it—my life and what it was to be was *my* responsibility. I had looked to every outside source, believing, even in coming to Karen that something, somewhere would finally provide the answer I needed.

Until now, I had only identified with the problem—never its solution. But Karen had changed all that. Now it was up to me.

9

When I first went to visit Karen Pitico in June of 1987, I was living a life that, for lack of a better definition, was simply no life at all.

Unable to control my moods and compulsive behavior patterns, I had ultimately fallen victim to them. Being a victim of oneself means that there is no longer anyone to pilot the ship—the ship simply drifts here and there, without purpose or direction. While engulfed in such a state, it is impossible to forecast what you will be doing, where you will be, even *who* you will be on any given day. Since I had no way of knowing how I might feel or what I might be capable of doing on a date several weeks in advance, I made no plans, no appointments, no commitments.

For those whose lives are well-structured and relatively predictable, it might be difficult to imagine the sort of quandary that makes it impossible to know if you will really be able to go to a party, visit a friend, attend a job interview, or even go to the store when the time to do such things finally arrives. In my own case, I decided the best way to avoid having to "cancel out" would be to not make any plans to begin with.

I had been working for CIGNA Healthplan of Arizona on a part-time basis. Twenty hours per week was all I could manage, and often even that was a struggle. After an entire day of binging, I would fall out of bed the following morning, overpowered by nausea and self-disgust as I tried to motivate myself and organize my day. I saw each day as a burden—as something to survive and get behind me as quickly as I could. But staying at home did not particularly appeal to me either. I hated housework and found it difficult to function with any sort of domestic efficiency except for those times when I was suddenly overpowered by one of my more manic moods. Then, with a frenetic burst of energy, I would attack the house, attempting to do everything at once. Afterwards, I would feel totally drained, and sometimes remain in bed for a period of several days.

An aerobics class I occasionally attended afforded some exposure to other people, but not often, for I found it impossible to adhere to any sort of regular schedule. Fortunately, no one seemed to care how often or how seldom I participated in the class, which spared me a lot of awkward explanations.

I had not thought of my life in any particular way until, with Karen's help, I finally took the time to examine it. Then, I was appalled at how dull and pointless everything was. Or had been. And very possibly might continue to be unless some dramatic changes took place.

I did not think of these changes as anything I might be able to influence or bring about. It seemed to me that I had already done all I could in trapping myself into this suffocating habit of going nowhere, doing nothing, and thinking about things as little as

112

I could. Had I been able to do more, I would surely have done it.

Karen did not agree. She asked how I thought I would live if every conceivable option were suddenly open to me—if I had all the drive, self-confidence and determination that were needed.

"You mean one of those the-sky's-the-limit situations?" I asked.

She nodded.

It was hard for me to imagine such a scenario after having felt trapped for such a long period of time. But, of course, if I were really able to do whatever I wanted . . if I were given those choices . . if those avenues were suddenly open to me . . . .

By the end of our conversation, I had begun to understand that most of the restrictions I labored under were only in my mind. I was only trapped because I had programmed myself to feel trapped. Which meant that if I changed the program to something else—to something that enabled me to feel unshackled, unburdened by yesterday's emotional baggage—if I were actually free to be whatever I chose to be, why then—yes, I might still have a chance.

In July, a cardiologist who regularly referred patients to my husband, asked if he thought I might be interested in doing some dietary consulting for her. When Larry mentioned this to me, I thought long and hard about it. Beginning to feel the old programmed responses which, as always, were urging me to immediately reject the idea, I called to arrange an appointment. It was only after several attempts that I finally managed to make contact. Afterwards, I was amazed at my own persistence. Prior to my introduction to Cognitive Therapy, I knew I would only

113

have called this woman once. I was pleased to discover this new streak of assertiveness in myself, and as time went on, grew increasingly curious with where it might lead. Before anything was even finalized I attended a party with Larry and joyfully told my friends about my new job. On the way home, Larry turned to me and said somewhat angrily, "You shouldn't have mentioned the job. It's not final yet. What if something goes wrong and you don't end up working there?"

Not long before, I would have begged for his forgiveness and retreated into my old belief system. Instead, I realized that Larry was merely telling me what would have been right for him. Karen helped me see that I could either *accept, reject, ignore* or *use* someone else's opinion. In any case, it didn't have to become my own. I found I was suddenly comfortable with telling Larry that it was okay for me to share my joy with my friends and that I would accept the consequences, even if they weren't what I had hoped for. Taking this step was a major turning point for me—understanding Larry's point of view, yet still being free to have my own!

In the case of the cardiologist, it led to my establishing a private practice out of her office. I saw my first patient on August 6, 1987, and greatly encouraged by this, decided to test the waters a bit more.

I composed a letter of introduction which I mailed to doctors in the Phoenix/Scottsdale area, and within a week, received my first response. A group of five cardiologists expressed an interest in having me consult with them a half-day each week. Soon, I was also consulting with a home health care agency, and a physician in the Carefree area.

With so many sudden and dramatic changes in my life, I did not immediately realize that my obsessive binging seemed to have stopped. When at last I did realize it, I wondered if such a thing were actually possible after only ten weeks of Cognitive Therapy. Although I was inclined to doubt it, there was no denying that my eating habits had changed. I was no longer taunted by packages of cookies, peanuts, candy or potato chips in the house. They continued to sit on the shelf, and as the days passed, there was no sudden frantic urge to tear into them and consume whatever was there.

One day I found myself wondering what it would be like to have a closet of clothes that were all the same size. In the past, my wardrobe had always consisted of three different sizes.

As I considered all the pleasant ramifications of maintaining my weight—of eating normal portions, of looking and feeling good, and living with some measure of consistency and control in my life—I felt as if I were standing poised at the edge of a miracle. If only it would happen! Unbeknownst to me, it already had.

On August 17, 1987, I did, in fact, succumb to my last attack of binge eating. At the time, I did not know it was the last, but it was.

Moral of the Story: I had never really had an eating disorder problem—not in the sense that I could not control my overpowering love for food. However I felt about food had little, if anything, to do with it. The entire time I had been feeding an ungovernable appetite, I had, in fact, been feeding my lack

115

of self-confidence, my loss of self-esteem, my indecisiveness, my inability to take charge of my life. Now that I had begun doing these things, the desire for food was falling away.

This was to be a major turning point in my life, a time when I was finally willing to accept what Cognitive Therapy had accomplished.

"You're accomplishing it yourself," Karen insisted. "Taking control of your thoughts, refusing to feed yourself bad information, taking an active interest in what happens rather than just making the best of things—that's what's made the difference, Dorie. A method of therapy has no power in itself. First, it must be diligently and constructively applied."

I listened as she spoke, wanting desperately to believe her. At that stage, it was still difficult for me to take credit for anything. I did not see myself as any kind of super-achiever. I had always admired such people, almost as if they were an alien race, for truly, I felt that we were worlds apart. But now I was being told that I was such a person too. Or that I had such capabilities. It was an exciting and challenging thought.

On days when I thought of myself as a goer—a doer, I found I accomplished much more than I usually did. This gave undeniable credence to one of the things I had learned through my therapy sessions— that my actions were, in fact, filtered through my feelings, which meant that how I felt would inevitably determine what I chose to do.

For all the years that I had felt badly about myself, I had managed to reinforce these feelings through a great many negative actions. But now that

I felt good about myself, my actions had had to adjust themselves accordingly.

I felt GOOD about myself!

Yes, it was true. It was becoming difficult to remember the last dark and gloomy time—the last thing I had been angry, confused or depressed about.

For all the years that my moods had controlled me, it had never once occurred to me that I might have the power to control them. Always, I had allowed myself to be buffeted about—like a straw in the wind, like a ship on the rocks (which I very nearly was). Suicide and Death. I had once actually considered those dreadful options!

Looking back on it, it seemed as if my thoughts were of somebody else, someone I had once known well, but not well enough to identify with.

If it was possible to make that much of a psychological transition, what else might eventually prove possible for me?

The answer was less than a month away. One day, I was contacted by a friend who explained that a woman she knew was looking for someone to cook for her family. I soon discovered that any number of people were desirous of obtaining such a service. Busy mothers and career women liked the idea of having someone else prepare nutritious evening meals rather than having to do this themselves, as did people on restricted diets, and others who simply enjoyed the luxury of having such a service provided.

Soon, I was operating a small catering service appropriately named 'Simply Supper' which enabled me to try my wings as an entrepreneur. Expecting to feel overwhelmed by the responsibilities and pressures involved, I was surprised to find that I not only enjoyed my work, but that I took a tremendous amount of pride in it.

In October of 1987 I studied hard in order to pass a national exam in order to become a certified diabetic educator.

After that, I aggressively sought more effective methods of promoting 'Simply Supper,' which included joining a women's networking group to help me promote this service.

As I undertook each step, which inevitably led to the next, it occurred to me that I was attempting things I could never have done only a year or so earlier.

And on a more personal level, I was learning to relate to my husband in a frank and honest manner. Whenever he annoyed me or made me feel unhappy, I immediately told him about it, no longer allowing my mood to fester and grow. There was never a backlash, as I had once feared there might be, but rather a sincere effort on Larry's part to understand and relate to my feelings.

How simple it all was! How simple it might have been all along! Outside of myself, there was no one else to blame for all the complications in my life, but then it had taken quite a while to understand how thought processes actually work.

Every idea that comes into our minds, every thought and feeling we have, is inevitably tied to something else that came before. In that sense, it is extremely difficult to have a so-called 'virgin' thought, for we generally have some preconceived notion that will tend to affect that thought, causing us to label it as either good or bad.

Since I had gotten into the habit of thinking badly of myself, it was hard to see anything commendable in my repeated efforts to change, to discipline or to cure myself of all that I felt to be wrong. And yet I had earnestly tried, which was quite an achievement in itself. Actually, I had never given up through all the absurd diet and exercise programs I had attempted and eventually abandoned. Why had I not been able to recognize the gargantuan effort involved, to at least credit myself with that quality of wanting to change, of wanting it so desperately that I would subject myself to anything I felt was necessary in order to achieve my ends?

I certainly hadn't been devoid of good intent or determination. And while it was true that I often did bad things, it wasn't because I was a bad person.

My image of myself was really all that had changed—my image and my ability to see things in a better, more positive light. Whatever happened now, whatever went wrong or failed to materialize as planned, was a situation outside myself. I had learned how to stand apart from the things that were happening, realizing that they weren't really happening to me.

Example: Let us assume that you hope to drive to the mountains in a half-hour but find that it actually takes an hour. What has happened is that all sorts of causes came together and crossed over to make it an hour. They included the weather, a detour, your state of mind which determined your driving speed, and so on. A thousand definite but unseen factors added up to make the result what it was. But no one deliberately conspired against you to make you late, or at least later than you had planned.

To understand something as simple and basic as this is to free yourself from needless anger and frustration which do nothing whatever to change the situation, and will only make you tense and unhappy.

Another thing it is important to learn is how to constructively deal with a problem. Again, it is important to place yourself outside the situation in order to remain truly objective.

Don't think of it as YOUR problem, but only as A problem.

DON'T SAY: If I don't soon make my next car payment, I'll face repossession.

SAY: There is a bill coming due that will soon be seriously delinquent unless something is done.

DON'T SAY: I'm such a coward! I don't have the guts to stand up for my own rights.

SAY: There is a fear of confronting another and causing a confrontation. How can it be handled?

Do you see the difference?

Choosing exactly how you will think about your problems is the first step in solving them. You'll win far more of your battles once you've learned to drop the "I," "me" and "mine."

Also, instead of looking at problems as catastrophes, try to see them as challenges. Concentrate only on the opportunity aspect of the battle. Focus your attention upon how much better things will be once the problem has been resolved.

In doing this, if it seems that you are playing little tricks on yourself, resorting to little mind games in order to "con" yourself into believing that life is actually much better than it is, you might wish to consider the possibility that it really IS better.

During the last half of 1987 I continued to see my therapist, Karen Pitico, on a weekly basis, and throughout that period, noticed at least a 70 percent improvement in my life. Yet, the world had not changed. And the circumstances and situations that surrounded me each day were essentially the same. But now the 'coping mechanism' had changed. I had begun to learn how to properly evaluate a problem, and to arrive at a logical solution without becoming overly emotional in the process. I no longer entertained the thought that life was against me. Life simply was. And whatever it required, I felt totally qualified and prepared to give.

In November, I was told by my supervisor at CIGNA that some major changes were taking place in our department. As a consequence, I was to be transferred out of the Health Education Department into the Diabetes Referral Program. This meant that my schedule would be radically changed, and the communities of Glendale and Sun City, which I would now be servicing, were much farther away, necessitating additional driving time. Then too, I would be losing so many of the patients I had grown extremely fond of.

On my next visit to her office, Karen and I discussed this unexpected turn of events.

"Exactly what is it about this situation that most upsets you?" she asked.

"The fact that I have no control over it, I guess."

"And have you considered the options available to you?"

I admitted I hadn't, that I was too upset.

"Well, why don't we do that now?" Karen urged.

The options, of course, were either to adapt to the situation as it was, or else, to quit my job. But quitting was not so easy—not as simple as walking into someone's office and saying those fateful words. The job was important to me in the sense that it helped me to structure my life. I knew I could hardly afford to slip back into the habit of simply drifting along from one day to the next.

"I think I'll just go along with this for now," I finally said, at which point Karen nodded and smiled. She had helped me to realize that I needed to give this new situation a chance. After all, I wasn't locked into the job. I could always leave if things didn't work out.

In the past, I had assumed that anything I said or did was automatically irrevocable. Once the die was cast, I believed myself to be hopelessly committed, which, in fact, had never been the case.

Although I was somewhat disturbed to realize that I still possessed a tendency to over-react, I managed to take consolation in the fact that I no longer over-reacted as a matter of course. The fact was, once I clearly understood the situation, and my automatic responses to it, it was relatively easy to resolve my problems. Slowly but surely, I was learning not to become emotionally involved. Then too, I had trained myself to remain on guard for 'unacceptable thoughts,' ones which had no function in my life except to distress me and drag me down.

Over the holidays, I was quite busy, experiencing the customary pressures that go with entertaining family and friends. Even so, I did not feel overpowered by any unusual amount of anxiety or stress. I felt well and happy, and ready for all that life had to offer.

In May of 1988, I became sick with a cold and spent several days in bed. Much to my alarm, I suddenly found myself overeating, and since I was too sick to exercise, I immediately sank into a fit of depression.

As quickly as I could, I once again met with Karen, pouring out my heart to her in a way that clearly revealed my panic.

"Don't worry," I was surprised to hear her say. "It's all part of the trilogy syndrome. Staying in bed caused you to make certain automatic associations— that of binging and of being depressed. For you, these things have always gone together. But this time you had a legitimate reason for staying in bed. You were sick. And now you are better. And that's all there is to it."

Amazed at the simple logic in this, I could already feel my fears subsiding. What a relief it was to know I didn't have to fall back into my old behavior patterns. It wasn't required! And so, I simply wouldn't do it! This was to be one of the most significant things that I would ever learn through Cognitive Therapy. The situation wasn't in control. I was!

123

Since that time, it has become easier and easier to identify and thus avoid the trilogy syndrome. I no longer feel that one negative experience will automatically lead to the next, and the fact is, it never has.

10

In April 1988 our house was robbed.

Returning from an errand, I did not immediately notice anything wrong, but then I saw the components of our stereo system randomly strewn about and realized I had surprised someone in the act of committing a burglary.

I was relieved at the thought that nothing had been taken, and that I had managed to avoid the thieves. A while later, I discovered that my engagement ring was missing, and although we were insured, I was devastated at this loss. Ultimately, the ring could be replaced with another toward which I felt no sentimental attachment, and while this was certainly better than nothing, I knew it would never be the same.

After the insurance claim had been filed, I resolved to put the matter out of my mind. Concentrating on all I had learned in Cognitive Therapy, I was determined to keep things in their proper perspective. I was quite pleased with my calm and reasonable attitude, which lasted all of five weeks. At the end of that time, I finally gave in to a wave of impatience and called my insurance agent to learn why my claim had not yet been processed.

The agent said he was unaware of all the details involved but that he would check into it. As part of the same conversation, he warned that I might not be reimbursed for the full value of the ring.

I was extremely incensed at this, and our conversation quickly deteriorated into a lot of senseless banter. When I hung up the phone, I knew nothing more than I had known before placing the call, but now, I was genuinely upset.

When Larry came home that evening, he was immediately subjected to my somewhat frenzied state, but managed to take it in stride. And why not? The entire scenario was not exactly new to him. In the past, I had often involved him in my daily frustrations, which I quickly compounded by adding ever more fuel to the fire.

In this particular instance, I railed on about our insurance claim, and then quickly moved on to other things.

"I think it was probably a mistake to start up my own business," I said. "I'm really not knowledgeable enough to make a success of it. And this book I've been trying to write. Well, I know it's beyond my capabilities. And even if I finish it, there's no guarantee that it will ever sell."

Larry listened as I ranted on.

"Nothing good ever happens in my life!" I finally insisted, then waited for him to contradict me.

I looked at Larry.

Larry looked at me.

All-or-Nothing Thinking was the phrase that immediately came to mind. Everything I had been saying was a prime example of it.

126

Once I had taken the time to apologize to Larry, I went into another room and sat down to think.

What was the actual problem here?

The problem concerned itself with an unresolved insurance claim. Nothing else. Only that.

What were my options?

Either I could accept a smaller settlement than the one I had anticipated, and buy a ring with that—or, I could save up the difference in order to make a more suitable purchase.

Those were my options. There was really nothing else to concern myself with.

When the insurance check finally arrived, I was amazed to find that it was actually for more than the appraised value of my ring. Once again, I had been stewing over nothing.

But I had not totally regressed. A year or so earlier, the same situation would have caused me to take to my bed, hopelessly overpowered by an impenetrable cloak of depression. This time, that hadn't happened.

Was I making progress? Apparently so. Would it continue? Yes! I was determined that it would.

Soon after the burglary, yet another traumatic incident occurred. One morning, a young man presented himself at my door, asking to use the phone. He explained that he was having mechanical problems with his car and that he needed to call a garage.

I directed him to a telephone in the hall, then returned to what I was doing in the kitchen.

A short while later, I looked up to see this same young man standing in the kitchen doorway. Looking toward me with an odd smile, he began to make a number of lewd suggestions.

I realized at once how foolish I had been to admit him into the house. Stories of accidents and car trouble were common ploys. I had read about other women being taken in by such tales. Now it had happened to me.

As the man attempted to back me up against a wall, I erupted in sudden anger.

"First my house gets robbed!" I screamed at the top of my lungs. "Then the insurance company takes five weeks to settle! And now THIS!"

Grabbing him by the arm, I quickly propelled him toward the door. I have no doubt that I succeeded in my efforts only because I had taken him by surprise. Once he was outdoors, I immediately locked the door and then called the police.

It was not until later in the day that I felt the full impact of this frightful experience. Returning home from a trip to the store, I found I could not bring myself to go back into the house. I sat in my car until Larry arrived, then told him exactly what had happened.

We talked outside until I was finally ready to accept that I was harboring an irrational fear in assuming that the man had returned and was back inside the house. At that, we came indoors and my anxieties gradually abated.

Once I was able to reflect upon this incident with greater objectivity, I was amazed at my own assertive behavior. It was difficult to say what had provoked me to oppose my would-be assailant with such vehemence and anger. Yet, I had done it—and once again, felt no need to take to my bed and stay there.

Without question, I had been making progress in the area of actions and reactions. Gradually, I was coming to terms with the fact that events did not really control me. It was actually my responses to the things that happened that either made or destroyed my day.

For a time, I thought long and hard about ignoring outside influences and becoming my own motivator. To believe that deeply in myself was to believe in the one individual who would never fail me. I found this to be a comforting thought, notwithstanding the fact that I had once had no confidence in this person, believing her to be without value, and beyond hope.

To become properly motivated is to invite a thorough analysis of the motivators that already exist. Everything from seductive atmospheres, and people, to billboards along the road. They all have something to sell.

Exactly what are you willing to buy?

In answering this question for myself, I have no choice but to recognize my own faulty thinking. On the subject of dieting alone, I could assail the reader with endless accounts of erroneous thinking. But then I had a great deal of help!

For Example:

In a recent newspaper ad for a diet center, a young woman attests to the fact that her motivation for losing weight is her husband — a handsome, professional man for whom she feels she MUST look good.

Upon reading this ad, I was tempted to take issue with it although I would once have strongly supported its faulty concept.

Consider for a moment what actually occurs when your strongest motivators exist in someone else. What happens if this person suddenly rejects you? Do you think you might then abandon your diet and begin to neglect your appearance? The possibility is certainly there, particularly if you are inclined to blame yourself for losing the man of your dreams.

People who feel at fault often feel the need to punish themselves. In the case of a chronic dieter, what do you suppose that punishment might be?

The only motivation that lasts, and the only kind you can trust is internal motivation. This is the kind that causes you to act in your own best interests, prompting you to strive toward a happier, healthier you.

And what of the diet itself? What does it consist of, and what does it require you to do?

For as long as you feel threatened by food, and fearful of losing all control, you may be sure you have not resolved the basic problem associated with over-eating.

The fact is, you must first reach a point where you feel comfortable around food, knowing you can eat as others do—sensibly and in moderation.

We were MEANT to eat, to eat those nutritious and delicious foods so essential to our health.

At a time when I ate poorly—either sparingly or in excessive amounts, I felt as threatened by food as anyone possibly could. I too avoided food, but this never resolved the problem. I was still living in a world where food was readily available, and where it soon became available to me.

Today, I am no longer tempted, even over-powered by the sight of food. I am not constantly preoccupied with the thought of it, and there is no way in which it constitutes a threat. I know I can eat sensibly as well.

I have stopped dieting and begun managing myself.

I have become my own motivator.

I am finally free.

OTHER HABITS AND HOW THEY GROW

This is not a diet book, but rather a book on how negative habits are formed. Overeating is one, smoking is another, and the list goes on and on.

Everywhere we look, we find people engaged in counter-productive habits that they would like to change. People who procrastinate, who squander their time, who find it impossible to save.

However one habit may differ from another, the source of that habit will not, for we are all a product of what we think, and how we think will determine what we do.

1. MENTAL PROGRAMMING DETERMINES OUR BELIEFS. At the outset—at the point where the habit originates, there is a programmed message that is constantly being played. Over and over, it repeats its negative theme.

"I've always been fat."

"I've never been lucky in love."

"There aren't enough hours in the day."

"I've never been artistically inclined."

Assuming you are currently in the clutches of a habit you would like to break, how would you summarize your present feelings about it? In the space provided below, write down your HONEST OPINION of yourself as it relates to a negative habit. Now then, what capabilities do you feel are needed to overcome such a habit? Do you feel that you possess these, or that you lack them?

Note: Please be totally honest in your answer!

Fear - I'm afraid I'm going to eat it nite

I tell myself I'm not going to do this

but I'm afraid that I will anyway -

and then, often I will do it. - I feel

like a weakling - but also confused -

why do I do this when I don't want

to? - I need calmness, motivation

or discipline to direct my feeling elsewhere

Yes -

132

Read aloud what you have written here and listen to the way it sounds. Bear in mind that this is the programmed message you are currently feeding into yourself and that it is this program that is governing your beliefs!

How do you feel about the things you have been saying to yourself? Do you find them helpful and inspiring? Again, I urge you to be totally honest in your answer.

If you are like most people, you may be appalled at many of the things you have been telling yourself. Perhaps you are wondering how you have even managed to function with somebody constantly kicking you in the teeth and tearing you down. More's the pity that you have been doing this to yourself!

Question: Just what good has it done? What have you accomplished in the course of constantly blaming and punishing the best friend you'll ever have? And why do you suppose you have been doing this?

2. BELIEFS CREATE ATTITUDES. The mental programming that has created your beliefs is, in fact, the first in a five-step process. Once beliefs have been formed and adopted, they create specific attitudes.

In the handwritten summary you have already composed, you may detect certain attitudes. You may wish to review it again with this in mind.

An attitude, by definition, is that which reflects our disposition, feelings, and moods. It is the posture we assume because of our basic beliefs.

In the following space, describe your current disposition, your prevalent feelings and moods. How would you describe your body language, the manner

remember all the things she cards—
to remember if she were left alone on
a desert island to live — she'd think of all kinds of

in which you stand, walk and sit? Do you have a confident stride, a spring in your step, a posture that is erect and proud? Do you gesture with confidence and authority, display a smiling countenance, exude sincerity and warmth? Whatever you convey through personal appearance and actions, please be truthful in writing it down.

I am often fighting discouragement

with myself + the world. I worry a lot when

I'm by myself — afraid I won't get things done or

can't get a good job etc. When I'm with others,

I'm perky & cheerful, but alone I'm lazy, sloppy, whiney

humorless — I walk FAST because I'm

worried that I won't get things done. I

don't gesture with authority — I gesture wishy-

washy — I am warm & sincere

(left margin) I know I'm warm and like people and living things — they interest + excite me — I need to remember — I really love them — I trust Jo Ann more — I need to be more confident + trust Jo Ann more — a lot — I need to be more confident —

134

However you rated yourself, it is likely that you see some room for improvement. Back in my "binge-eating" days, my own disposition, feelings and moods were all firmly rooted in a cloud of chronic depression. I looked and felt terrible, and once I became a walking testimonial for these negative attitudes, I quickly adopted the habits of an isolationist, spending much of my time in bed. Although your own behavior patterns may be less extreme, you can be sure that they are an accurate indication of the way you feel about yourself. This is because:

→ *frightened* *out of control* *lack of confidence in self regarding manipula... tng*

3. ATTITUDES CREATE FEELINGS. How do you actually feel? When you awaken each morning, are your spirits high? Do you feel optimistic and cheerful—mentally challenged by the work that lies ahead? *no* In personal relationships, do you feel both loved and loving? *Jim too critical* Are you content with what you have, and grateful for each new day? *no* In the space provided below, describe exactly how you feel about yourself, your loved ones, and life in general.

I usually feel bad about myself - like I need a lot of improvements - I'm especially mad that I don't just get free and get creative and make my own lifestyle by working with less than ideal - un-cluttered, complicated conditions & obstacles (like KIDS - BILL etc) I am mad and critical & judgmental of my kids and Bill - though I really like them and I WANT them around. I used to believe life was exciting & colorful I wanted to experience & feel & see & do everything I could. Then I decided I was blocked with the KIDS (instead of working them into the pattern, and I have (weakly) adopted an attitude re: life in general is that it's disappointing, difficult, often very drudgery

_____

_____

_____

_____

_____

✳ Take particular note of any feelings of vague dis-
content, any unexplainable blue moods or periods of
depression. There is a reason for everything you feel!
Quite often, it is the feelings we deliberately suppress
that cause us the greatest difficulty. At the time that
I was suffering from a severe eating disorder, I was
also suppressing deep-seated feelings of anger and
resentment. I had always believed that such feelings
were unacceptable, that I must never allow myself to
acknowledge or express them. It was this sort of
thinking that eventually led to my confinement in a
mental institution, and it was there that I finally
learned how to properly acknowledge and evaluate
my feelings.

   4. **FEELINGS DETERMINE ACTIONS.** A
kindly old lady who takes in stray pets is acting on
her feelings. So is a mass-murderer whose feelings of
anger and frustration have become so totally over-

whelming that he is now compelled to annihilate the world. Whatever your feelings, they will inevitably dictate a course of action. In the space provided below, make a list of specific feelings that have caused you to behave in specific ways. At this juncture, do not concern yourself with whether or not your actions were appropriate, logical, or even rational. Just itemize them, then take note of the various feelings that brought these actions about.

FEELINGS	ACTIONS
Tired, leg hurt, not much to do	drank 2 beers
Tired, sick of girls fighting	got really mad +
Angry, don't know what to do or how to stop girls, feel responsible,	yelled A7 girls — even physically blocked Beth
Felt happy	exercised A7 ypma
rushed - wanted to get Mom's Phone call over -	phoned mom WAS snotty to her

In the foregoing list, you may have noticed that you often acted in ways that you later regretted.

137

"If I hadn't been so angry, I never would have said that."

"I can't believe I actually made such a scene."

"I must have been out of my mind!"

Are you beginning to see the intricate relationship that exists between Programming-Beliefs-Attitudes-Feelings and Actions? Yes, one irrevocably leads to the next. And finally, we have:

5. RESULTS. Results are the actual outcome, something we may or may not have wanted to achieve. As the last link in the chain, results are the culmination of everything that came before.

In the space provided below, list the outcome of various actions you have taken, paying close attention to what it was you originally sought to achieve, and what you actually accomplished.

Example: I intend to lose a pound per week over a period of thirteen weeks.

Did you do it? What was the final result?

ACTION/INTENDED ACTION   RESULT

ACTION/INTENDED ACTION	RESULT
ate / intended to diet	gained or stayed same
half-way cleaned shower / clean shower	only clean a little
straighten up clean house	went to bed

_____

_____

_____

_____

_____

In cases where you did not achieve the desired result, what do you feel was the reason?

Your attitude? Your feelings? Your beliefs?

No! It all began with your original programming, whatever message you first fed into yourself, from which your beliefs, attitudes, feelings and actions were ultimately formed.

If dieting was actually the problem, consider how the problem first began.

Example of Bad Programming:

"I've got to lose some weight."

How much? Your subconscious mind will not act on so vague an instruction. And anything you "lose" you may one day "find" again, so forget about losing. Think about BEING thin, as a goal already achieved.

IN SUMMARY: Whatever you hope to accomplish, it all begins with programming. For good or for bad, you become what you are programmed to believe.

Begin today to take charge of your thoughts.

Stand guard over every idea.

Once you have learned to manage your mind, you will be able to control what goes into it.

GARBAGE IN—GARBAGE OUT
IS THAT WHAT LIFE IS ALL ABOUT?

Let's hope not!

You CAN reach your goals, and achieve all your dreams.

AND TODAY IS THE DAY TO BEGIN!

◆ ◆ ◆ ◆

140

11

Is there any way to KNOW if the unhappiness and frustration you are currently experiencing are products of a thinking disorder?

If you are presently overweight, is there any way to determine if the problem is really something other than food?

Whatever the situation, I would urge you to look a little deeper than the problem itself—for there is certainly something that is causing it.

A simple test that you can take in the privacy of your own home concerns itself with five basic questions:

1. Do I arrive at a conclusion based upon one small detail of a situation rather than looking at the entire picture?
☑ Yes   ☐ No

2. Do I arrive at decisions without ample supportive evidence—in other words, am I merely assuming?
☐ Yes   ☐ No

3. Do I categorize experiences into rigid autonomies such as all good or all bad?
☑ Yes   ☐ No

4. Do I over- or under-value the significance of events or circumstances?
☑ Yes   ☐ No

5. Do I relate events to myself when, in fact, there is no real basis for making this connection?
☑ Yes   ☐ No

In reviewing your answers, would you say that any of them fall into the categories listed below?

1. Exaggerating
2. Ignoring the positive
3. Personalizing (believing that everything revolves around you)
4. Either/Or (Either you achieve your goal or you are a total failure)
5. Overgeneralization (Seeing yourself only in negative terms—believing nothing ever turns out right)

If you do, in fact, constantly subject yourself to faulty thinking, you may be sure that your self-esteem and self-image have begun to suffer accordingly. The way you see yourself and the way you feel about yourself are inextricably linked—and the end result is the way in which you perceive the world.

It is truly unfortunate that so many of us are governed by our own distorted perceptions—not at all by the way things are, but by the way we happen to see them.

What has caused this to happen? Why do we feel as we do?

Once again, I would like you to take a little test. (Please answer as honestly as you can!)

TRUE or FALSE

	T	F
1. Do you carry burdens that really belong to others?	✓	
2. Do you behave in a helpless manner?	✓	
3. Do you wait for good times to happen rather than creating them for yourself?	✓	
4. Do you believe it is wrong to become angry?	✓	
5. Do you blame others for your difficulties in life?	✓	
6. Do you expect others to make you happy?		✓
7. Do you expect others to meet your needs?		✓
8. Do you let others rule your life?	✓	
9. Are you inclined to ask people to do things for you?		✓
10. Do you vocalize your opinions?		✓
11. Is there a certain amount of give-and-take in your significant relationship with others?		✓
12. Do you make a lot of negative statements to yourself about your life, your job, and family?	✓	
13. Do you look at the facts or only make assumptions before arriving at a decision?	✓	
14. Are you aware of your assumptions?		✓
15. Do you engage in a lot of anticipating?	✓	

16. Do you believe that luck guides your life? ✓ ____
17. Do you avoid decision-making and encourage others to dominate you? ✓ ____
18. Do you often view yourself as a victim? ✓ ____
19. Do you tend to think in all-or-nothing terms? ✓ ____
20. Do you create options and alternatives for yourself? ____ ✓
21. Do you think about and remind yourself of your strengths? ✓ ✗ ____
22. Have you learned to grow through our pain and sorrow? ✓ ____
23. Do you find it hard to forgive? ____ ✓
24. Is it important to you to be liked?
25. Are you extremely concerned with what other people think about you? ✓ ____
26. Do you tend to label situations and events that do not go the way you would like for them to? ✓ ____
27. Have you stopped growing, expanding and evolving? ____ ✓

In addition to the foregoing, please answer the following questions in your own words:

28. What do you do when someone is not there for you?

I feel mad and SAD and feel like they don't
care about me + help is hard — sometimes I eat

144

29. What do you do with your anger?

I try to deflect it - avoid it -
but I'm going to start verbalizing it
+ then expressing it in private

30. What do you want and need for yourself?

I need freedom to choose my lifestyle
and approach to life - while incorporating
weaving, including my loved ones into it -

31. Are you living in the past, present, or future?
    In what way?

future – I think about what

I need to do while not changing

anything in the present

32. Do you have any great passions in your life?

No – not right now

33. How badly do you want to feel good about
    yourself?

A LOT

Although you may be displeased or even shocked
with some of your answers, you will probably feel
somewhat enlightened as well.

It is important to realize that before you can make any progress in life, you must first determine where you are.

Where you are and where you want to be may have little in common. Perhaps your goals in life are so ill-defined that you do not even know what they are.

What does this tell you about yourself?

Could it be telling you that you have never quite accepted that you are even entitled to anything?

If this is the case, do not despair. As your negative thinking gradually changes, as it becomes more positive and self-rewarding, you will begin to have some very definite thoughts and ideas about things:

. . . Who you are
. . . Where you are going
. . . What you want out of life ?
. . . And Why?

Let us assume that you would one day like to be rich. If that is the case, are you comfortable with that goal—or do you sometimes feel the need to justify it?

Many people feel guilty about wanting to be rich. They associate such a desire with greed, even as others fret over the complications and changes that money may bring into their lives.

What they really fear is their own inability to cope with a new situation, perhaps because of a poor self-image and low self-esteem.

Let's look at a few healthy affirmations on the subject of wealth, as they might be voiced by an individual who not only knows what he wants but also knows himself:

I WANT TO BE RICH:

1. So that I can work in my chosen field, providing a (product/service) that is of value to others
2. To purchase a new home
3. To buy a recreational vehicle
4. To travel
5. To help others
6. To have a retreat—in the mountains or by the sea
7. To purchase a better wardrobe
8. To further my education
9. To alleviate stress over money
10. To enjoy greater independence

I DESERVE TO BE RICH BECAUSE:

1. I am talented
2. I am dedicated
3. I am willing to work
4. I am well-intentioned
5. I have repeatedly demonstrated courage and initiative
6. I am entitled to a long, stress-free life
7. I am a nice person—a good person
8. I have genuine childlike enthusiasm
9. I have repeatedly demonstrated patience and optimism in the face of much adversity
10. I have satisfactorily fulfilled my obligations to others

Do you find yourself agreeing with what this person wants—but only for him, not for you?

When applied to you, are you uncomfortable with such statements as: "I am a nice person—a good person"—"I am talented"—"I am entitled . . ."

Are you beginning to see your true self-image? And the way it is working against you? Do you see how it defeats you in advance, before you even have a chance to prove yourself? Before you even try?

Using the same format shown above, create a list of your own, related to something you want and feel you deserve.

I WANT: _money_

1. Relieve stress

2. Give girls & Bill things they want

3. To travel

4. help others

5. To live comfortably — by ocean

6. Independence

7.

8.

9.

10.

I DESERVE _money_
BECAUSE:

1. Work hard

2. Have talent

3. Am decent

4. Work well with people

5. Genuinely care about quality
   of product I give to others

6.

7.

8.

9.

10.

Did you have a problem completing these lists? Was it more difficult to determine what you want, or to convince yourself that you truly deserve it?

Would you like to feel differently about yourself, your life, and the things you are entitled to? *yes*

It's easier than you think.

All you need to do is to accept that you and you ALONE are in charge of the way you want to feel.

You actually have that power.

You actually have that choice.

Make the decision to do what you choose and you have taken your first independent step.

You did it once before—when you were very small.

You took that first step . . and then another . . and yet another.

And after that, the world got in the way.

But only because you allowed it.

What of tomorrow?

Are you willing to acknowledge that you create your own reality—that you are responsible for whatever occurs?

Whatever it is, you are making it happen, both good and bad.

What would you LIKE to have happen?

Potentially speaking, you already ARE the person you have always wanted to be.

There is no further need to live in darkness. Darkness, after all, is not real. It is merely a lack of light. Turn on the light and the darkness immediately vanishes.

Control your thoughts and you will control your circumstances.

Why? Because proper thoughts always lead to proper actions.

The choice is yours.

Turn on the light!

❖ ❖ ❖ ❖

Epilogue

It is unfortunate that feelings of low self-esteem and low self-identity are so common, shared by millions in our country, a country that purports to be one of the wealthiest in the world, financially wealthy perhaps, but not emotionally.

Emotionally, millions of Americans are stressed out, are unable to cope with their problems, feel inadequate in their jobs and in their relationships. They are dissatisfied with their family, friends and also with themselves. While life in the 90s should be challenging, interesting and exciting, millions of people dread each day. Despite great strides in research and public awareness during the past twenty years, anxiety and depression are commonplace.

While some depression has its roots in chemical imbalances—feelings of hopelessness, worthlessness, and low self-esteem are the products of learned negative thinking habits.

Through Cognitive Therapy, or "Thinking Therapy" it is possible to learn positive thought habits and routines. We do this by learning the proper way to "think" about things rather than simply reacting by rote.

Unfortunately, many people have developed unhealthy, negative thinking processes which guarantee failure at something, whether it be meeting new people, learning a new task or confronting a spouse.

"I never have any luck meeting someone new." "We always get into an argument." "I'm so clumsy and slow that I know I won't be able to learn this task. I can't do anything right." "Nobody likes me." We have programmed ourselves and become trapped by our own negative thinking habits. Yes, this mental programming is learned and reinforced every time we experience everyday situations. The problem is we stay trapped in this negative thinking because we don't have, nor have we learned, appropriate thinking tools.

When I met Dorie on June 18, 1987, I listened to her describe herself. She made numerous negative statements. I asked her, "Why are you saying all these negative things about yourself?" She replied, "Because they are true." She believed them to be true, and so they were. Dorie and I began weekly counseling sessions. One of the first "thinking tools" I urged her to adopt involved the question, *"What are my options?" "Do I have to think like this?"*

An early issue was her binge eating. She had labelled (or programmed) herself a binge eater. I asked her if it was the binging itself or her learned negative thinking habits which kept her a binge eater? She thought about this, and during the next session she said, "You're right. I don't have to binge."

"Yes," I told her, "You do have choices and you do have options."

Over the next year Dorie and I discussed many of her life experiences. She began to learn more appropriate thinking tools to deal with her life experiences. She began to use common sense, to look at her options and create options that supported a positive outlook. She began to meet her needs and take care of herself.

It is truly unfortunate that our educational system provides us with the opportunity to learn math and science, to read and write and spell, but does not show us how to take care of ourselves emotionally, to cope, to be happy, to get what we want out of life. Consequently, many of us reach adulthood without knowing how to take care of our emotional needs.

Cognitive Therapy teaches us to think creatively about ourselves, to fulfill our personal needs and wants by using common sense, and by developing thinking tools to support us throughout out lives.

So many times my clients will say, "I have to please, to help, to satisfy my boss, spouse, friends, children and peers." We tend to please and satisfy everyone's needs but our own. And at our own expense. We build up anger, resentment and emotional pain when our needs and wants are overlooked or not met.

Dorie and I have outlined many thinking tools fundamental to people who want to feel good about themselves. By properly applying them, we can learn to solve, cope and develop options leading to a happier inner and outer self.

It is my sincere wish that those of you searching for a better, happier life will investigate Cognitive Therapy. It has much to offer the person seeking freedom from depression, low self-esteem and low self-image. Happy thinking!

Karen D. Pitico M.A. ACSW

Order Form

Everybody's Doing It...
And Here's How to Quit
by Dorie F. Pass R.D.

Send to: Golden One Publishing
         P.O. Box 44542
         Phoenix, AZ 85064-4542

Name_____

Address_____

City_____State_____Zip_____

Send $12.95 for each book ordered. Add $2.00 for shipping and handling. Arizona residents please add .84 sales tax.

Number of books _____ x $12.95   _____
Shipping   _____ x   2.00   _____
Tax   _____ x   .84   _____
Amount enclosed   _____

Allow 4 weeks for delivery.